COMPREHENSIVE RESEARCH
AND STUDY GUIDE

John Ashbery

BLOOM'S MAJOR POETS

EDITED AND WITH AN INTRODUCTION
BY HAROLD BLOOM

CURRENTLY AVAILABLE

John
Ashbery

CHELSEA HOUSE
PUBLISHERS
A Haights Cross Communications Company

Philadelphia

BLOOM'S *MAJOR*
POETS

EDITED AND WITH AN INTRODUCTION
BY HAROLD BLOOM

© 2004 by Chelsea House Publishers, a subsidiary of
Haights Cross Communications.

A Haights Cross Communications ◤ Company

Introduction © 2004 by Harold Bloom.

Printed and bound in the United States of America.

First Printing
1 3 5 7 9 8 6 4 2

Library of Congress Cataloging-in-Publication Data

John Ashbery / edited and with an introduction by Harold Bloom.
     p. cm. — (Bloom's major poets)
  Includes bibliographical references and index.
  ISBN 0-7910-7887-6
  1. Ashbery, John—Criticism and interpretation. I. Bloom, Harold. II.
Series.
  PS3501.S475Z73 2003
  811'.54—dc22

                                                    2003024088

Chelsea House Publishers
1974 Sproul Road, Suite 400
Broomall, PA 19008-0914

http://www.chelseahouse.com

Contributing Editor: Michael Baughan

Cover design by Keith Trego

Layout by EJB Publishing Services

CONTENTS

USER'S GUIDE

This volume is designed to present biographical, critical, and bibliographical information on the author and the author's best-known or most important poems. Following Harold Bloom's editor's note and introduction is a concise biography of the author that discusses major life events and important literary accomplishments. A critical analysis of each poem follows, tracing significant themes, patterns, and motifs in the work. As with any study guide, it is recommended that the reader read the poem beforehand and have a copy of the poem being discussed available for quick reference.

A selection of critical extracts, derived from previously published material, follows each thematic analysis. In most cases, these extracts represent the best analysis available from a number of leading critics. Because these extracts are derived from previously published material, they will include the original notations and references when available. Each extract is cited, and readers are encouraged to check the original publication as they continue their research. A bibliography of the author's writings, a list of additional books and articles on the author and their work, and an index of themes and ideas conclude the volume.

ABOUT THE EDITOR

Harold Bloom is Sterling Professor of the Humanities at Yale University and Henry W. and Albert A. Berg Professor of English at the New York University Graduate School. He is the author of over 20 books, and the editor of more than 30 anthologies of literary criticism.

Professor Bloom's works include *Shelley's Mythmaking* (1959), *The Visionary Company* (1961), *Blake's Apocalypse* (1963), *Yeats* (1970), *A Map of Misreading* (1975), *Kabbalah and Criticism* (1975), *Agon: Toward a Theory of Revisionism* (1982), *The American Religion* (1992), *The Western Canon* (1994), and *Omens of Millennium: The Gnosis of Angels, Dreams, and Resurrection* (1996). *The Anxiety of Influence* (1973) sets forth Professor Bloom's provocative theory of the literary relationships between the great writers and their predecessors. His most recent books include *Shakespeare: The Invention of the Human*, a 1998 National Book Award finalist, *How to Read and Why* (2000), *Stories and Poems for Extremely Intelligent Children of All Ages* (2001), *Genius: A Mosaic of One Hundred Exemplary Creative Minds* (2002), and *Hamlet: Poem Unlimited* (2003).

Professor Bloom earned his Ph.D. from Yale University in 1955 and has served on the Yale faculty since then. He is a 1985 MacArthur Foundation Award recipient and served as the Charles Eliot Norton Professor of Poetry at Harvard University in 1987–88. In 1999 he was awarded the prestigious American Academy of Arts and Letters Gold Medal for Criticism. Professor Bloom is the editor of several other Chelsea House series in literary criticism, including BLOOM'S MAJOR SHORT STORY WRITERS, BLOOM'S MAJOR NOVELISTS, BLOOM'S MAJOR DRAMATISTS, BLOOM'S MODERN CRITICAL INTERPRETATIONS, BLOOM'S MODERN CRITICAL VIEWS, BLOOM'S BIOCRITIQUES, BLOOM'S GUIDES, BLOOM'S MAJOR LITERARY CHARACTERS, and BLOOM'S PERIOD STUDIES.

EDITOR'S NOTE

My Introduction brings together a series of meditations on John Ashbery's poetry that I published in the decade 1972–1982. Essentially, I read Ashbery as the legitimate heir of Walt Whitman and of Wallace Stevens.

As this volume contains twenty-seven critical views upon six poems of Ashbery, I will comment here upon only a few representative interpretations.

On "Soonest Mended," Charles Berger, John Hollander, and Vernon Shetley offer rather Formalist readings of a poem clearly able to sustain them.

David Kalstone, Lee Edelman, and Thomas Gardner all attempt to clear away some of the paradoxes of "Self-Portrait in a Convex Mirror."

"Wet Casements," a poem at once lucid and difficult, is perspectivized usefully by David Bromwich and Karen Mills-Courts.

The amazing Orphic elegy, "Syringa," is foregrounded by John Shoptaw, the scholar most fully versed in Ashbery's sources and manuscripts.

I am particularly moved by the deep analyses that the poet James Applewhite gives to "A Wave," and by the distinguished critic Helen Vendler's exegesis of "At North Farm."

Harold Bloom

In the exquisite squalors of Tennyson's "The Holy Grail," as Percival rides out on his ruinous quest, we can experience the hallucination of believing that the Laureate is overly influenced by *The Waste Land*, for Eliot too became a master at reversing the *apophrades*. Or, in our present moment, the achievement of John Ashbery in his powerful poem "Fragment" (in his volume *The Double Dream of Spring*) is to return us to Stevens, somewhat uneasily to discover that at moments Stevens sounds rather too much like Ashbery, an accomplishment I might not have thought possible.

The strangeness added to beauty by the positive *apophrades* is of that kind whose best expositor was Pater. Perhaps all Romantic style, at its heights, depends upon a successful manifestation of the dead in the garments of the living, as though the dead poets were given a suppler freedom than they had found for themselves. Contrast the Stevens of "Le Monocle de Mon Oncle" with the "Fragment" of John Ashbery, the most legitimate of the sons of Stevens:

> Like a dull scholar, I behold, in love,
> An ancient aspect touching a new mind.
> It comes, it blooms, it bears its fruit and dies.
> This trivial trope reveals a way of truth.
> Our bloom is gone. We are the fruit thereof.
> Two golden gourds distended on our vines,
> Into the autumn weather, splashed with frost,
> Distorted by hale fatness, turned grotesque.
> We hang like warty squashes, streaked and rayed,
> The laughing sky will see the two of us,
> Washed into rinds by rotting winter rains.
> (—"Le Monocle," VIII)

> Like the blood orange we have a single
> Vocabulary all heart and all skin and can see
> Through the dust of incisions the central perimeter
> Our imaginations orbit. Other words,

Old ways are but the trappings and appurtenances
Meant to install change around us like a grotto.
There is nothing laughable
In this. To isolate the kernel of
Our imbalance and at the same time back up carefully
Its tulip head whole, an imagined good.

(—"Fragment," XIII)

An older view of influence would remark that the second of
these stanzas "derives" from the first, but an awareness of the
revisionary ratio of *apophrades* unveils Ashbery's relative triumph in
his involuntary match with the dead. This particular strain, while
it matters, is not central to Stevens, but is the greatness of Ashbery
whenever, with terrible difficulty, he can win free to it. When I
read "Le Monocle de Mon Oncle" now, in isolation from other
poems by Stevens, I am compelled to hear Ashbery's voice, for this
mode has been captured by him, inescapably and perhaps forever.
When I read "Fragment," I tend not to be aware of Stevens, for his
presence has been rendered benign. In early Ashbery, amid the
promise and splendors of his first volume, *Some Trees*, the massive
dominance of Stevens could not be evaded, though a *clinamen* away
from the master had already been evidenced:

The young man places a bird-house
Against the blue sea. He walks away
And it remains. Now other

Men appear, but they live in boxes.
The sea protects them like a wall.
The gods worship a line-drawing
Of a woman, in the shadow of the sea
Which goes on writing. Are there
Collisions, communications on the shore

Or did all secrets vanish when
The woman left? Is the bird mentioned
In the waves' minutes, or did the land advance?

(—"Le Livre est sur la Table," II)

This is the mode of *The Man with the Blue Guitar*, and

urgently attempts to swerve away from a vision whose severity it cannot bear:

> Slowly the ivy on the stones
> Becomes the stones. Women become
>
> The cities, children become the fields
> And men in waves become the sea.
>
> It is the chord that falsifies.
> The sea returns upon the men,
>
> The fields entrap the children, brick
> Is a weed and all the flies are caught,
>
> Wingless and withered, but living alive.
> The discord merely magnifies.
>
> Deepe within the belly's dark,
> Of time, time grows upon the rock.
> (—"The Man with the Blue Guitar," XI)

The early Ashbery poem implies that there are "collisions, communications among us, even in confrontation of the sea, a universe of sense that asserts its power over our minds. But the parent-poem, though it will resolve itself in a similar quasi-comfort, harasses the poet and his readers with the intenser realization that "the discord merely magnifies," when our "collisions, communications" sound out against the greater rhythms of the sea. Where the early Ashbery attempted vainly to soften his poetic father, the mature Ashbery of "Fragment" subverts and even captures the precursor even as he appears to accept him more fully. The ephebe may still not be mentioned in the father's minutes, but his own vision has advanced. Stevens hesitated almost always until his last phase, unable firmly to adhere to or reject the High Romantic insistence that the power of the poet's mind could triumph over the universe of death, or the estranged object-world. It is not every day, he says it his *Adagia*, that the world arranges itself in a poem. His nobly desperate disciple, Ashbery, has dared the dialectic of misprision so as to implore the world daily to arrange itself into a poem:

> But what could I make of this? Glaze
> Of many identical foreclosures wrested from
> The operative hand, like a judgment but still
> The atmosphere of seeing? That two people could
> Collide in this dusk means that the time of
> Shapelessly foraging had come undone: the space was
> Magnificent and dry. On flat evenings
> In the months ahead, she would remember that that
> Anomaly had spoken to her, words like disjointed beaches
> Brown under the advancing signs of the air.

This, the last stanza of "Fragment," returns Ashbery full circle to his early "Le Livre est sur la Table." There are "collisions, communications on the shore" but these "collide in this dusk." "Did the land advance?" of the early poem is answered partly negatively, by the brown, disjointed beaches, but partly also by "the advancing signs of the air." Elsewhere in "Fragment," Ashbery writes: "Thus reasoned the ancestor, and everything / Happened as he had foretold, but in a funny kind of way." The strength of the positive *apophrades* gives this quester the hard wisdom of the proverbial poem he rightly calls "Soonest Mended," which ends by:

>   ... learning to accept
> The charity of the hard moments as they are doled out,
> For this is action, this not being sure, this careless
> Preparing, sowing the seeds crooked in the furrow,
> Making ready to forget, and always coming back
> To the mooring of starting out, that day so long ago.

Here Ashbery has achieved one of the mysteries of poetic style, but only through the individuation of misprision.

II

Another misprision is a haunting lyric of belatedness, Ashbery's recent "As You Came from the Holy Land," where the parodistic first-line/title repeats the opening of a bitter ballad of lost love attributed to Ralegh, one of whose stanzas lingers throughout Ashbery's gentler poem:

> I have lovde her all my youth,
>   Butt now ould, as you see,
> Love lykes not the fallyng frute
>   From the wythered tree.

"Her" is the personal past in Ashbery's elegy for the self:

> of western New York state
> were the graves all right in their bushings
> was there a note of panic in the late August air
> because the old man had peed in his pants again
> was there turning away from the late afternoon glare
> as though it too could be wished away
> was any of this present
> and how could this be
> the magic solution to what you are in now
> whatever has held you motionless
> like this so long through the dark season
> until now the women come out in navy blue
> and the worms come out of the compost to die
> it is the end of any season
>
> you reading there so accurately
> sitting not wanting to be disturbed
> as you came from that holy land
> what other signs of earth's dependency were upon you
> what fixed sign at the crossroads
> what lethargy in the avenues
> where all is said in a whisper
> what tone of voice among the hedges
> what tone under the apple trees
> the numbered land stretches away
> and your house is built in tomorrow
> but surely not before the examination
> of what is right and will befall
> not before the census
> and the writing down of names

remember you are free to wander away
as from other times other scenes that were taking place
the history of someone who came too late
the time is ripe now and the adage
is hatching as the seasons change and tremble
it is finally as though that thing of monstrous interest
were happening in the sky
but the sun is setting and prevents you from seeing it
out of night the token emerges
its leaves like birds alighting all at once under a tree
taken up and shaken again
put down in weak rage
knowing as the brain does it can never come about
not here not yesterday in the past
only in the gap of today filling itself
as emptiness is distributed
in the idea of what time it is
when that time is already past

Ashbery, probably because of his direct descent from Stevens, tends like Stevens to follow rather precisely the crisis-poem paradigm that I have traced in my map of misreading. This model, Wordsworthian-Whitmanian, never restores as much representational meaning as it continually curtails or withdraws, as I have observed earlier. Ashbery's resource has been to make a music of the poignance of withdrawal. So, in this poem, the "end of any season" that concludes the first stanza is deliberately too partial a synecdoche to compensate for the pervasive absences of the ironies throughout the stanza. Ashbery's turnings-against-the-self are wistful and inconclusive, and he rarely allows a psychic reversal any completeness. His origins, in the holy land of western New York state, are presented here and elsewhere in his work with an incurious rigidity that seems to have no particular design on the poet himself, characteristically addressed as "you." The next stanza emphasizes Ashbery's usual metonymic defense of isolation (as opposed to the Stevensian undoing or the Whitmanian regression), by which signs and impulses become detached from one another, with the catalog or census completing itself in the reductive "writing down of names," in which "down" takes on surprising difference and force. The third stanza, one of Ashbery's most radiant, marks the poem's *daemonization*, the American Counter-Sublime in which Ashbery, like Stevens, is so extraordinarily at home. Ashbery's mingled strength and weakness, indeed his deliberate pathos, is that he knowingly begins where Childe Roland ended, "free to wander away" yet always seeing himself as living "the history of someone who came too late" while sensing that "the time is ripe now." Studying his own habitual expression in his prose *Three Poems*, he had compared himself explicitly to Childe Roland at the Dark Tower. Here also, his Sublime sense that a Stevensian reality is happening in the war of the sky against the mind is necessarily obscured by a sunset akin to Roland's "last red leer."

Ashbery's finest achievement, to date, is his heroic and perpetual self-defeat, which is of a kind appropriate to conclude this book, since such self-defeat pioneers in undoing the mode of transumption that Stevens helped revive. Ashbery's allusiveness is transumptive rather than conspicuous, but he employs it against itself, as though determined to make of his lateness a desperate cheerfulness. In the final stanza of *As You Came from the Holy Land*, the most characteristic of Shelleyan-Stevensian metaphors, the fiction of the leaves, is duly revealed as a failure ("taken up and shaken again / put down in weak rage"); but the metalepsis substituted for it is almost a hyperbole of failure, as presence and the present fall together "in the gap of today filling itself / as emptiness is distributed." The two lines ending the poem would be an outrageous parody of the transumptive mode if their sad dignity were not so intense. Ashbery, too noble and poetically intelligent to subside into a parodist of time's revenges, flickers on "like a great shadow's last embellishment."

III

Ashbery has been misunderstood because of his association with the "New York School" of Kenneth Koch, Frank O'Hara and other comedians of the spirit, but also because of the dissociative phase of his work as represented by much of a peculiar volume, *The Tennis Court Oath*. But the poet of *The Double Dream of Spring* and the prose *Three Poems* is again the Stevensian meditator of the early *Some Trees*. No other American poet has labored quite so intensely to exorcise all the demons of discursiveness, and no contemporary American poet is so impressively at one with himself in expounding a discursive wisdom. Like his master, Stevens, Ashbery is essentially a ruminative poet, turning a few subjects over and over, knowing always that what counts is the mythology of self, blotched out beyond unblotching.

Ashbery's various styles have suggested affinities to composer-theorists like Cage and Cowell, to painters of the school of Kline and Pollock, and to an assortment of French bards like Roussel, Reverdy and even Michaux. But the best of Ashbery, from the early *Some Trees* on through "A Last World" and "The Skaters" to the wonderful culminations of his great book, *The Double Dream of Spring* and the recent *Three Poems*, shows a clear descent from the major American tradition that began in Emerson. Even as his poetic father is Stevens, Ashbery's largest ancestor is Whitman, and it is the Whitmanian strain in Stevens that found Ashbery. I would guess that Ashbery, like Stevens, turned to French poetry as a deliberate evasion of continuities, a desperate quest for freedom from the burden of poetic influence. The beautiful group called "French Poems" in *The Double Dream of Spring* were written in French and then translated into English, Ashbery notes, "with the idea of avoiding customary word-patterns and associations." This looks at first like the characteristic quarrel with discursiveness that is endemic in modern verse, but a deeper familiarity with the "French Poems" will evoke powerful associations with Stevens at his most central, the seer of "Credences of Summer":

> And it does seem that all the force of
> The cosmic temperature lives in the form of contacts
> That no intervention could resolve,
> Even that of a creator returned to the desolate
> Scene of this first experiment: this microcosm.
>
> ... and then it's so natural
> That we experience almost no feeling
> Except a certain lightness which matches

The recent closed ambiance which is, besides
Full of attentions for us. Thus, lightness and wealth.

But the existence of all these things and especially
The amazing fullness of their number must be
For us a source of unforgettable questions:
Such as: whence does all this come? and again:
Shall I some day be a part of all this fullness?

The poet of these stanzas is necessarily a man who must have absorbed "Credences of Summer" when he was young, perhaps even as a Harvard undergraduate. Every strong poet's development is a typology of evasions, a complex misprision of his precursor. Ashbery's true precursor is the composite father, Whitman-Stevens, and the whole body to date of Ashbery's work manifests nearly every possible revisionary ratio in regard to so formidable an American ancestry. Though the disjunctiveness of so much of Ashbery suggests his usual critical placement with the boisterousness of Koch or the random poignances of O'Hara, he seems most himself when most ruefully and intensely Transcendental, the almost involuntary celebrator "of that *invisible light* which spatters the silence / Of our every-day festivities." Ashbery is a kind of invalid of American Orphism, perpetually convalescing from the strenuous worship of that dread Orphic trinity of draining gods: Eros, Dionysus, Ananke, who preside over the Native Strain of our poetry.

I propose to track Ashbery back to his origins in another essay, but here I have space only to investigate some poems of his major phase, as it seems developing in his two most recent books. To enter at this point a judgment of current American poets now entering their imaginative maturity, Ashbery and A. R. Ammons are to me the indispensable figures, two already fully achieved artists who are likely to develop into worthy rivals of Frost, Stevens, Pound, Williams, Eliot, Crane, and Warren. Merwin, James Wright, Merrill, perhaps Snyder in the school of Williams and Pound, perhaps James Dickey of a somewhat older generation (if he yet returns to the strength of earlier work) are candidates also. Yet all prophecy is dangerous here; there are recent poems by Howard, Hollander, Kinnell, Pack, Feinman,

Hecht, Strand, Rich, Snodgrass, among others, which are as powerful as all but the very best of Ammons, Ashbery, Wright. Other critics and readers would nominate quite different groupings, as we evidently enter a time of singular wealth in contemporary verse.

Ashbery's poetry is haunted by the image of transparence, but this comes to him, from the start, as "a puzzling light," or carried by beings who are "as dirty handmaidens / To some transparent witch." Against Transcendental influx, Ashbery knows the wisdom. of what he calls "learning to accept / The charity of the hard moments as they are doled out," and knows also that: "One can never change the core of things, and light burns you the harder for it." Burned by a visionary flame beyond accommodation (one can contrast Kinnell's too-easy invocations of such fire), Ashbery gently plays with Orphic influx ("Light bounced off the ends / Of the small gray waves to tell / Them in the observatory / About the great drama that was being won."). Between Emerson and Whitman, the seers of this tradition, and Ashbery, Ammons and other legatees, there comes mediating the figure of Stevens:

> My house has changed a little in the sun.
> The fragrance of the magnolias comes close,
> False flick, false form, but falseness close to kin.
>
> It must be visible or invisible,
> Invisible or visible or both;
> A seeing and unseeing in the eye.

These are hardly the accents of transport, yet Stevens does stand precariously, in the renewed light. But even the skepticism is Emerson's own; his greatest single visionary oration is *Experience*, a text upon which Dickinson, Stevens and Ashbery always seem to be writing commentaries:

> Thus inevitably does the universe wear our color, and every object fall successively into the subject itself. The subject exists, the subject enlarges; all things sooner or later fall into place. As I am, so I see; use what language we will, we can never say anything but

what we are.... And we cannot say too little of our constitutional necessity of seeing things under private aspects, or saturated with our humors. And yet is the God the native of these bleak rocks.... We must hold hard to this poverty, however scandalous, and by more vigorous self-recoveries, after the sallies of action, possess our axis more firmly....

The Old Transcendentalism in America, like the New, hardly distinguishes itself from a visionary skepticism, and makes no assertions without compensatory qualifications. Still, we tend to remember Emerson for his transparencies, and not the opaquenesses that more frequently haunted him and his immediate disciples. I suspect that this is because of Emerson's *confidence*, no matter where he places his emphases. When Stevens attains to a rare transparence, he generally sees very little more than is customary, but he *feels* a greater peace, and this peace reduces to a confidence in the momentary capability of his own imagination. Transcendentalism, in its American formulation, centers upon Emerson's stance of Self-Reliance, which is primarily a denial of the anxiety of influence. Like Nietzsche, who admired him for it, Emerson refuses to allow us to believe we must be latecomers. In a gnomic quatrain introducing his major essay on self-reliance, Emerson manifested a shamanistic intensity still evident in his descendents:

Cast the bantling on the rocks,
Suckle him with the she-wolf's teat,
Wintered with the hawk and fox,
Power and speed be hands and feet.

This is splendid, but Emerson had no more been such a banding than any of my contemporaries are, unless one wants the delightful absurdity of seeing Wordsworth or Coleridge as a she-wolf. "Do not seek yourself outside yourself" is yet another motto to *Self-Reliance*, and there is one more, from Beaumont and Fletcher, assuring us that the soul of an honest man:

Commands all light, all influence, all fate
Nothing to him falls early or coo late.

These are all wonderful idealisms. Whitman, who had been simmering, read *Self-Reliance* and was brought to the boil of the 1855 "Song of Myself." Ashbery, by temperament and choice, always seems to keep simmering, but whether he took impetus from Whitman, Stevens or even the French partisans of poetic Newness, he has worked largely and overtly in this Emersonian spirit. Unfortunately, like Merwin and Merwin's precursor, Pound, Ashbery truly absorbed from the Emerson-Whitman tradition the poet's over-idealizing tendency to lie to himself, against his origins and against experience. American poets since Emerson are all antithetical completions of one another, which means mostly that they develop into grotesque truncations of what they might have been. Where British poets swerve away from their spiritual fathers, ours attempt to rescue their supposedly benighted sires. American bards, like Democritus, deny the swerve, so as to save divination, holding on to the Fate that might make them liberating gods. Epicurus affirmed the swerve, ruining divination, and all poetry since is caught between the two. Emerson, though close to Democritus, wants even divination to be a mode of Self-Reliance. That is, he genuinely shares the Orphic belief that the poet is already divine, and realizes more of this divinity in writing his poems. Lucretian poets like Shelley who find freedom by swerving away from fathers (Wordsworth and Milton, for Shelley) do not believe in divination, and do not worship an Orphic Necessity as the final form of divinity. Orphic poets, particularly American or Emersonian Orphics, worship four gods only: Ananke, Eros, Dionysus and—most of all surely—themselves. They are therefore peculiarly resistant to the idea of poetic influence, for divination—to them—means primarily an apprehension of their own possible sublimity, the gods they are in process of becoming. The gentle Ashbery, despite all his quite genuine and hard-won wisdom, is as much in this tradition as those spheral men, Emerson, Whitman, Thoreau, and that sublime egoist, Stevens, or the American Wordsworth.

The Double Dream of Spring has a limpidly beautiful poem called "Clouds," which begins:

All this time he hod only been waiting,
Not even thinking, as many had supposed.
Now sleep wound down to him as its promise of dazzling peace
And he stood up to assume that imagination.

There were others in the forest as close as he
To caring about the silent outcome, but they had gotten lost
In the shadows of dreams so that the external look
Of the nearby world had become confused with the cobwebs inside.

Sleep here has a Whitmanian-Stevensian cast ("The Sleepers," "The Owl in the Sarcophagus") and the gorgeous solipsism so directly celebrated here has its sources in the same ultimately Emersonian tradition. Though "he," the poet or quest-hero, is distinguished from his fellows as not having yielded to such solipsism, the poem ends in a negative apotheosis:

He shoots forward like a malignant star.
The edges of the journey are ragged.
Only the face of night begins to grow distinct
As the fainter stars call to each other and are lost.

Day re-creates his image like a snapshot:
The family and the guests are there,
The talking over there, only now it will never end.
And so cities are arranged, and oceans traversed,

And farms tilled with especial care.
This year again the corn has grown ripe and tall.
It is a perfect rebuttal of the argument. And Semele
Moves away, puzzled at the brown light above the fields.

The harvest of natural process, too ripe for enigmas, refutes quest, and confirms the natural realism of all solipsists. This poem, urging us away from the Emersonian or Central Self, concludes by yielding to that Self, and to the re-birth of Dionysus, Semele's son. Like his precursor, Stevens, Ashbery fears and evades the Native Strain of American Orphism and again like

Stevens he belongs as much to that strain as Hart Crane or John Wheelwright does. In the recent prose *Three Poems*, he ruefully accepts his tradition and his inescapable place in it:

> Why, after all, were we not destroyed in the conflagration of the moment our real and imaginary lives coincided, unless it was because we never had a separate existence beyond that of those two static and highly artificial concepts whose fusion was nevertheless the cause of death and destruction not only for ourselves but in the world around us. But perhaps the explanation lies precisely here: what we were witnessing was merely the reverse side of an event of cosmic beatitude for all except us, who were blind to it because it took place inside us. Meanwhile the shape of life has changed definitively for the better for everyone on the outside. They are bathed in the light of this tremendous surprise as in the light of a new sun from which only healing and not corrosive rays emanate; they comment on the miraculous change as people comment on the dazzling beauty of a day in early autumn, forgetting that for the blind man in their midst it is a day like any other, so that its beauty cannot be said to have universal validity but must remain fundamentally in doubt.
>
> (*The Recital*)

The closest (though dialectically opposed) analogue to this passage is the great concluding rhapsody of Emerson's early apocalypse, *Nature*, when the Orphic Poet returns to prophecy:

> As when the summer comes from the south the snow-banks melt and the face of the earth becomes green before it, so shall the advancing spirit create its ornaments along its park, and carry with it the beauty it visits and the sons, which enchants it; it shall draw beautiful faces, warm hearts, wise discourse, and heroic acts, around its way, until evil is no more seen. The kingdom of man over nature, which cometh not with observation,—a dominion such as now is beyond his dream of God,—he shall enter without more wonder than the blind man feels who is gradually restored to perfect sight.

Ashbery's apocalyptic transformation of the Self, its elevation to the Over-Soul, is manifest to everyone and everything outside the Self, but not to the blind man of the Self. The Emersonian Self will know the metamorphic redemption of others and things only by knowing first its gradual freedom from blindness as to its own glory. Ashbery's forerunners, the makers of *Song of Myself* and *Notes toward a Supreme Fiction*, were primary Emersonians, involuntary as Stevens was in this identity. Ashbery is that American anomaly, an antithetical Transcendentalist, bearer of an influx of the Newness that he cannot know himself.

IV

I leap ahead, past Frost and Pound, Eliot and Williams, past even Hart Crane, to a contemporary image-of-voice that is another strong tally, however ruefully the strength regards itself. Here is John Ashbery's "The Other Tradition," the second poem in his 1977 volume, *Houseboat Days*:

> They all came, some wore sentiments
> Emblazoned on T-shirts, proclaiming the lateness
> Of the hour, and indeed the sun slanted its rays
> Through branches of Norfolk Island pine as though
> Politely clearing its throat, and all ideas settled
> In a fuzz of dust under trees when it's drizzling:
> The endless games of Scrabble, the boosters,
> The celebrated omelette au Cantal, and through it
> The roar of time plunging unchecked through the sluices
> Of the days, dragging every sexual moment of it
> Past the lenses: the end of something.
> Only then did you glance up from your book,
> Unable to comprehend what had been taking place, or
> Say what you had been reading. More chairs
> Were brought, and lamps were lit, but it tells
> Nothing of how all this proceeded to materialize
> Before you and the people waiting outside and in the next
> Street, repeating its name over and over, until silence
> Moved halfway up the darkened trunks,
> And the meeting was called to order.
>   I still remember
> How they found you, after a dream, in your thimble bar,
> Studious as a butterfly in a parking for.

The road home was nicer then. Dispersing, each of the
Troubadours had something to say about how charity
Had run its race and won, leaving you the ex-president
Of the event, and how, though many of these present
Had wished something to come of it, if only a distant
Wisp of smoke, yet none was so deceived as to hanker
After that cool non-being of just a few minutes before,
Now that the idea of a forest had clamped itself
Over the minutiae of the scene. You found this
Charming, but turned your face fully toward night,
Speaking into it like a megaphone, not hearing
Or caring, although these still live and are generous
And all ways contained, allowed to come and go
Indefinitely in and out of the stockade
They have so much trouble remembering, when your forgetting
Rescues them at last, as a star absorbs the night.

I am aware that this charming poem urbanely confronts,
absorbs and in some sense seeks to overthrow a critical theory,
almost a critical climate, that has accorded it a canonical status.
Stevens's Whitman pro claims that nothing is final and that no
man shall see the end. Ashbery, a Whitman somehow more
studiously casual even than Whitman, regards the prophets of
belatedness and cheerfully insists that his forgetting or repression
will rescue us at last, even as the Whitmanian or Stevensian
evening star absorbs the night. But the price paid for this
metaleptic reversal of American belatedness into a fresh earliness
is the yielding up of Ashbery's tally or image of voice to a
deliberate grotesquerie. Sexuality is made totally subservient to
time, which is indeed "the end of something," and poetic tradition
becomes an ill-organized social meeting of troubadours, leaving
the canonical Ashbery as "ex-president / Of the event." As for the
image of voice proper, the Whitmanian confrontation of the
night now declines into: "You found this / Charming, but turned
your face fully toward night, / Speaking into it like a megaphone,
not hearing / Or caring." Such a megaphone is an apt image for
Paul de Man's deconstructionist view of poetic tradition, which
undoes tradition by suggesting that every poem is as much a
random and gratuitous event as any human death is.

Ashbery's implicit interpretation of what he wants to call *The Other Tradition* mediates between this vision, of poems as being totally cur off from one another and the antithetical darkness in which poems carry over-determined relationships and progress towards a final entropy. Voice in our poetry now tallies what Ashbery in his "Syringa," a major Orphic elegy in *Houseboat Days*, calls "a record of pebbles along the way." Let us grant that the American Sublime is always also an American irony, and then turn back to Emerson and hear the voice that is great within us somehow breaking through again. This is Emerson in his journal for August 1859, on the eve of being burned out, with all his true achievement well behind him; but he gives us the true tally of his soul:

> *Beatitudes of Intellect.*—Am I not, one of these days, to write consecutively of the beatitude of intellect? It is too great for feeble souls, and they are over-excited. The wineglass shakes, and the wine is spilled. What then? The joy which will not let me sit in my chair, which brings me bolt upright to my feet, and sends me striding around my room, like a tiger in his care, and I cannot have composure and concentration enough even to set down in English words the thought which thrills me—is not that joy a certificate of the elevation? What if I never write a book or a line? for a moment, the eyes of my eves were opened, the affirmative experience remains, and consoles through all suffering.

V

Of the many contemporary heirs of Whitman and of Stevens, John Ashbery seems likeliest to achieve something near to their eminence. Yet their uncertainty as to their audience is far surpassed in the shifting; stances that Ashbery assumes. His mode can vary from the apparently opaque, so disjunctive as to seem beyond interpretation, to a kind of limpid clairvoyance that again brings the Emersonian contraries together. Contemplating Parmigianino's picture in his major long poem, *Self-Portrait in a Convex Mirror*, Ashbery achieves a vision in which art, rather than nature, becomes the imprisoner of the soul:

The soul has to stay where it is,
Even though restless, hearing raindrops at the pane,
The sighing of autumn leaves thrashed by the wind,
Longing to be free, outside, lust it must stay
Posing in this place. It must move as little as possible.
This is what the portrait says.
But there is in that gaze a combination
Of tenderness, amusement and regret, so powerful
In its restraint that one cannot look for long.
The secret is too plain. The pity of it smarts,
Makes hot tears spurt: that the soul is not a soul,
Has no secret, is small, and it fits
Its hollow perfectly: its room, our moment of attention.

Whitman's Soul, knowing its true hour in wordlessness, is apparently reduced here and now to a moment only of attention. And yet even this tearful realization, supposedly abandoning the soul to a convex mirror, remains a privileged moment, of an Emersonian rather than Paterian kind. Precisely where he seems most wistful and knowingly bewildered by loss, Ashbery remains most dialectical, like his American ancestors.

The simple diction and vulnerable stance barely conceal the presence of the American Transcendental Self, an ontological self that increases even as the empirical self abandons every spiritual assertion. Hence the "amusement" that takes up its stance between "tenderness" and "regret," Whitmanian affections, and hence also the larger hint of a power held in reserve, "so powerful in its restraint that one cannot look for long." An American Orphic, wandering in the Emersonian legacy, can afford to surrender the soul in much the name temper as the ancient Gnostics did. The soul can be given up to the Demiurge, whether of art or nature, because a spark of *pneuma* is more vital than the *psyche*, and fits no hollow whatsoever. Where Whitman and Stevens are at once hermetic and off-hand, so is Ashbery, but his throwaway gestures pay the price of an ever-increasing American sense of belatedness.

John Ashbery

John Lawrence Ashbery was born July 28, 1927, in Rochester, New York and grew up on a fruit farm in nearby Sodus, a small community on the southern edge of Lake Ontario. His parents, Chester and Helen, had both earned college degrees; his father studied agriculture at Cornell University and became a farmer, and his mother taught biology at a nearby high school. Ashbery's biggest intellectual influence, however, came from his maternal grandfather, Henry Lawrence, a professor of physics who chaired the department at the University of Rochester, and in whose stimulating company and prodigious library young John spent a great deal of time. A literal "Quiz Kid" on the early radio program, Ashbery wrote his first poem at age eight. That same year, he began taking piano lessons and learned to read music, but his first love was painting, and he attended weekly classes at the Memorial Art Gallery in Rochester throughout his early teens. Thanks to a private grant from a neighbor, Ashbery was also able to attend Deerfield Academy, a prep school in Massachusetts, where he was first exposed to the poetry of W.H. Auden, Dylan Thomas, and Wallace Stevens. Though he never lost interest in art or music, Ashbery's greatest talent clearly lay in his way with the written word—two poems Ashbery wrote as a high school senior were later published in the prestigious *Poetry* magazine.

Ashbery spent his undergraduate years at Harvard, where he wrote perceptive studies of Stevens and Auden and became editor of the *Harvard Advocate*, publishing works of his own as well as by fellow poets and close friends Frank O'Hara and Kenneth Koch. He earned his B.A. in 1949 and went on to get a master's degree from Columbia in 1951, writing his thesis on Henry Green and specializing in French literature. For the next six years, Ashbery lived in New York City and engaged in a variety of creative activities while supporting himself as a copywriter for Oxford University Press and McGraw-Hill. In addition to many more poems, Ashbery wrote a pair of plays (*The*

Heroes and *The Compromise*), collaborated with James Schuyler on a satirical novel (*A Nest of Ninnies*), and acted in a Living Theater production of Picasso's *Desire Trapped by the Tail*. Significant influences during these journeyman years included Abstract Expressionism, the ego examinations of Andre Gide, the poetry of Elizabeth Bishop, and Ashbery's ongoing friendships and collaborations with O'Hara, Koch, and Schuyler. The last of these earned him a permanent association with the so-called "New York School" of poets, a somewhat limiting classification that he has since transcended.

Ashbery's first chapbook, *Turandot and Other Poems* (1953) received scant attention from critics and the public alike. A year or so later he collected what he considered his best work to date under the title of *Some Trees* and submitted the manuscript to the Yale Series of Younger Poets competition, judged that year by W.H. Auden. These early poems combine a formal rigidity (many are written in traditional, albeit playfully contrived, modes likes the pantoum, calzone, and sestina) with a surrealist obliqueness. They also display a clear debt to Stevens and Auden. Initially, Ashbery's and O'Hara's entries were rejected by screeners at Yale University Press, but Auden requested to see both after he was unsatisfied with the rest of the field and ultimately awarded Ashbery the prize, though not without some misgivings. *Some Trees* was published in 1956. By that time, Ashbery had moved to France under the auspices of a Fulbright Fellowship. With the exception of some additional graduate work in French literature at New York University from 1957–58, he lived in France (primarily Paris) for the next ten years, nine of which with French writer Pierre Martory. While there, he worked as an art critic for the European edition of the *New York Herald Tribune* and *Art International*, as well as Paris correspondent for *Art News*. Drawing inspiration from the revolutionary examples set by Gertrude Stein and French writers Raymond Roussel and Pierre Reverdy in literature, Willem de Kooning and Jackson Pollock in painting, and John Cage in music, and convinced by a continued lack of critical reception that his work would remain marginalized anyway, Ashbery began to experiment with disjointed syntax. Many of the results appeared in *The Tennis Court Oath*. Though it remains his most opaque work and the one many otherwise favorable critics discount as a failed aberration, *The Tennis Court Oath* proved to be a significant influence on many postmodern writers, particularly the so-called "Language" poets.

In 1966, shortly after the death of Frank O'Hara, Ashbery returned to the United States, took a position as Executive Editor of *Art News*, and published *Rivers and Mountains*. Though less consciously experimental and more accessible than *The Tennis Court Oath*, Ashbery's third collection nonetheless cemented his reputation as a "difficult" poet, prone to abstraction and solipsism. During the decade that followed, he also worked as an art critic for *New York* and *Newsweek* magazines, taught creative writing at Brooklyn and Bard Colleges, and published several more poetry collections. Beginning in 1970, with *The Double Dream of Spring*, Ashbery began to attract more attention from an academic establishment just coming to grips with the wave of avant-garde, free-associative verse dubbed "The New American Poetry" in the seminal 1960 anthology of the same name.

The long prose pieces that comprise *Three Poems* (1972) signaled another stylistic departure for Ashbery, away from his former elliptical approach and towards an expansive all-inclusiveness that often involved liberal use of vernacular and cliché. Critical and popular momentum for Ashbery's poetry culminated in 1975 when his next book of verse, *Self Portrait in a Convex Mirror*, won a Pulitzer Prize, a National Book Award, and a National Book Critics Circle Award. Buoyed by the acclaim, Ashbery churned out four poetry volumes (*Houseboat Days*, *As We Know*, *Shadow Train*, and *A Wave*) and a collection of drama (*Three Plays*) in quick succession. More accolades followed: Ashbery won a Bollingen Prize in 1984 and a MacArthur Prize in 1985. Hardly content to rest on his laurels, he has published over a dozen books since that time, including a collection of art criticism (*Reported Sightings*, 1989) and the six lectures he gave as the 1988–89 Charles Eliot Norton Professor of Poetry at Harvard (*Other Traditions*, 2000). Ashbery's later verse continues his program of experimentation and reinvention, textured and enriched by a keener sense of his own mortality and evermore canonized place in the postmodern poetic tradition.

Today, Ashbery divides his time between Manhattan and Hudson, New York. He is the Charles P. Stevenson, Jr., Professor of Languages and Literature at Bard College and the current Poet Laureate of New York. His latest work, *Chinese Whispers*, was published in 2002.

CRITICAL ANALYSIS OF
"Soonest Mended"

For several reasons, above and beyond the obvious merit of "Soonest Mended," introducing John Ashbery *in medias res*, with a poem from his fourth major collection, makes perfect sense. Ashbery himself begins almost all his works mid-thought, with one eye winking back at art and literary history, the other eye blinking rapidly in sync with the ever-accelerating pace of postmodern life, and a third, inner eye scanning the surreal landscape of the dream world. "Soonest Mended" is poised at the center point of this continuum. The title, initially cryptic, is resolved in the half-remembered aphorism "least said, soonest mended," a phrase that cuts through the poem and Ashbery's work as a whole with double-edged sharpness. It is also a poem about middle age (Ashbery was in his early forties at the time of its publication), about how to assess one's past and future without losing track of the present, and about taking stock and accepting one's limitations. Finally, though his first few collections earned Ashbery a reputation for stylistic innovation and fresh expression, it was only with the publication of *The Double Dream of Spring* (1970) that he began to emerge from a marginal, avant-garde existence and garner wider admiration. "Soonest Mended" also addresses that transition while elegizing what is lost in the process.

Apropos, the poem's first lines allude to the tenuous life of an experimental poet—"barely tolerated, living on the margin" and in apparent need of patronage from the sentries of the Ivory Tower, whose sometimes fickle bequeathments (such as the Yale Younger Poets prize awarded to Ashbery's first collection *Some Trees* by rear-guarde laureate W. H. Auden, who later admitted he hardly understood a word of it, or the Fulbright Fellowship that funded Ashbery's first trip to France) have the power to "rescue" struggling writers from the "brink of destruction." But these lines are also about anyone disenfranchised or alienated by "our technological society," anyone living paycheck to paycheck and grappling with the "daily quandary about food and the rent and bills to be paid." This ability to quickly cut from a private close-up to a more generalized, long view of contemporary consciousness is characteristic of Ashbery, as is his tendency for sudden shifts from the abstract to the specific, highbrow to lowbrow, elevated diction to vernacular cliché. Works of high art, such as Ariosto's 16th-century romantic epic *Orlando Furioso*, a scene from which is captured in Ingres's also-mentioned 19th-century painting *Roger Delivering Angelica*, coexist with the Happy Hooligan, an early comic-strip character. Both ends of the cultural spectrum are perfectly at home in Ashbery's poetry, "in a mind / with room enough and to spare," but he questions whether any of these creations, including his own poem, are capable of conveying "information." Ashbery imbues this generic word with a special, almost hermetic meaning that hides one of the keys not only to this poem but also his work as a whole—primarily an attempt to divine and articulate precisely that which is forever evading capture, like the "robin [that] flies across / The upper corner of the window," uncertainly perceived and gone before you can "brush your hair away" to confirm it was even there at all. What does seem clear is that the poem's speaker has arrived at a point where he feels the methods and motives, even the basic conception, that he and his peers (the ever-shifting pronouns "we," "you," and "us" reach out, in radiating spheres of scope, to include fellow New York School poets, poets everywhere, his readers, and the general populace) had been using to apprehend that "information," were faulty and misguided. The second half of the poem sets about trying to assimilate this new awareness.

Part of that assimilation requires turning tired life metaphors on their heads. The first is the obstacle "course," through which we dart and weave, braving the "hazards" to arrive at some finish line. The second is the "game," with its assumed "rules" and divisions between "players" and "spectators." The third is "college," an educational rite of passage that we supposedly complete to prepare ourselves for the real world. And the last is the most fundamental of all—the belief that aging brings wisdom. All are false models, says the poem, all misdirect by promising a definite resolution or point of epiphany. The harsh but beautiful truth of the matter is that "the course *was* hazards and nothing else," that "thinking not to grow up / Is the brightest kind of maturity" and "None of us ever graduates from college." And yet, these new models are also imperfect, lacking in any real "information" and essentially just left-handed restatements of the old protocol. In the end, the poem both acknowledges this fact ("though nothing / Has somehow come to nothing") and begrudgingly, though not without irony, accepts the necessity of social constructs ("the avatars / of our conforming to the rules … have made … 'good citizens' of us, / Brushing the teeth and all that"). The last six lines posit a final reformulation, employing oxymorons to convey the "information" that can only be gleaned by perpetually confronting and embracing life's paradoxes. For just as profound doubt is the sincerest form of belief, so too is "learning to accept / The charity of the hard moments" a kind of action and "making ready to forget" a mode of "careless" preparation.

It is precisely this process of thinking things through that most interests Ashbery. He is not *describing* contemplation, after the fact. Nor is he handing down any pre-packaged epiphanies. "Soonest Mended" recreates the *act* of contemplation, the constant groping about for "loose / Meaning, untidy and simple like a threshing floor." The undeniable tone of elegy expresses, on the one hand, nostalgia for those simpler years, "before it was time to start all over again," when being on the avant-garde (or simply living through the early years of postmodernism) was full of excitement and promise and the energizing ambition "to be small and clear and free" of the old ways of thinking. On the other hand, says the poem's concluding lines, perhaps there is something even more vital about not being sure—about constantly creating your life anew. By bottling this process of reconsideration in a poem that can be read and re-read years hence, Ashbery is creating a meta-model for life that will "always [be] coming back / To the mooring of starting out."

"Soonest Mended"

CHARLES BERGER ON ENDING AT THE BEGINNING

[Charles Berger is an Associate Professor of English at the University of Utah. In addition to many articles on contemporary literature, he is the author of *Forms of Farewell: The Late Poetry of Wallace Stevens* and co-editor of *James Merrill: Essays in Criticism*. In this extract, Berger maps the poem's "haphazard course" to the point of its origin.]

For too long Ashbery has seemed to readers—especially professional readers—a poet more often casual than relentless about establishing meaning. His mask of insouciance has managed to remain intact, despite the writing of poem after difficult poem, and the evidence is that each new effort has been aimed hard at getting his subject right—not fixing it forever, but bringing the moment's wisdom and the moment's ephemerality together. Too often, critics have stressed the latter and ignored the former. A myth grew up around Ashbery: he had somehow discovered new dimensions to the poetic act, or a new kind of writing machine, capable of generating poems in the absence of the usual anxieties about subject—more remarkably, poems free from worry about the traditional criteria of greatness. Ashbery has contributed to this myth in subtle ways, but supporters and critics have gone even further, sometimes suggesting that Ashbery had willed himself to be a minor poet, inhabitor of a necessarily diminished sphere. They seize on lines such as the following: "To step free at last, minuscule on the gigantic plateau— / This was our ambition: to be small and clear and free."

These lines come from "Soonest Mended," one of Ashbery's most popular poems. It is a poem written firmly in the middle voice and one which seems to erect an aesthetic credo out of holding to the middle range in all things: "a kind of fence-sitting / Raised to the level of an aesthetic ideal." The poem needs to be quizzed on this advocacy, however, if it does not indeed already question itself. One reason "Soonest Mended" is so well liked, aside from its wrought gracefulness and measured tone of loss, is that it gives an image of the poet many readers would like Ashbery to be: casual, urbane, resigned to "an occasional dream, a vision."

Now the poems we have been considering—"The Task," "Spring Day," "Evening in the Country," "Parergon"—are hardly what we would call conversational, although "Evening in the Country" comes closest perhaps to "Soonest Mended" in its use of the long line as a way of achieving flexibility of voice. Yet the conversational measure tightens toward the close of "Evening in the Country," and even though Ashbery keeps to an urbane pitch he manages to ascend the chariot of poetic deity. Readers are probably coming to realize that Ashbery has almost unobtrusively mastered the long line—the line of more than ten syllables—and now uses it as powerfully as anyone before him in the twentieth century. From *Double Dream* to *Houseboat Days* his power over this measure has only grown. The long line is also the visionary line, the mode of Whitman and Blake, and Ashbery has not been reluctant to use it in this task. The lengthened line, however, can trail away from the poet, as it does in "As I Ebb'd with the Ocean of Life," creating an effect of dispersed power and draining strength. Or the line can seem to hover in a kind of fruitful suspension, a creative sense of drift and repose. This feeling steals over one at times in reading Keats's odes, where the lines seem to grow longer than ten syllables as the Keatsian patience spreads its wings. "Soonest Mended" fulfills this last use of the long line almost perfectly, but it is worth noting that the poem is sui generis and not "vintage" Ashbery. More often, Ashbery will begin with a sense of drift but then gather toward some point of vision. The first poem in *Houseboat Days* is a perfect illustration. "Street Musicians" sees rising signs of drift but looks beyond them to what it perceives as a possible source, an "anchor": "Our question of a place of origin hangs / Like smoke."

"Barely tolerated, living on the margin," is something between a boast and a lament. The margin, once again, does not necessarily lead to marginality: it may be the true center. Yet

"Soonest Mended" is less sure than other Ashbery poems of the poet's power to be the center wherever he falls out, on the "brink" or what not. I would still argue that even as the poem's seemingly limpid lines crystallize with time and repeated readings, so its sense of marginality inches toward the center. Indeed, the movement is already there in the poem however one interprets it, for the margin of the poem's opening line becomes a "mooring" at the end. The precarious present yields to a sense of origins: the self is where it is as a result of an original event or choice. Our exile to the margin is self-willed. We started out from the margin-as-mooring; we are always placing ourselves by necessity at the brink of a new beginning, a making ready. Only when we lose the trace of the tether back to this site do we regard ourselves as weakly marginal. So the poem will move back through personal memory to an event *in illo tempore*, or sacred time, when the poet's true chronology began.

"Soonest Mended" remains striking within the Ashbery oeuvre not so much for its return at the end to a sense of origination—other poems certainly enact this course—as for its planned, haphazard course to that end. David Kalstone has written beautifully of this trajectory. He speaks of the poem's "brave carelessness" and points out, rightly, that "the tone is partly elegiac." Ashbery's suppression of mimesis only partly obscures the clear fact that "Soonest Mended" is, as Harold Bloom calls it, a lament for "Ashbery's generation." Writing at the level he does throughout *The Double Dream of Spring* inevitably means that Ashbery will feel deep ambivalence toward this comically helpless "generation" and toward his own early self. But I must disagree with Kalstone when he says that "'mooring' sounds as much like death as a new life." He tends to be more concerned with how the poem "shifts quickly from one historical hazard to another," while "the energetic lines breathe the desire to assert ego and vitality." As a stylistic description of the poem this cannot be surpassed.

"Historical hazard" is something Ashbery does not often open his poems to; the randomness of the ordinary is not quite the same thing. Such randomness can be organized and redeemed by the solitary eye; but history, or life within the community, can become far more oppressive to the poet. Ashbery's detractors would argue that he closes himself off to what he cannot organize, despite an appearance of the erratic within his poems, and this is hard to dispute. "Soonest Mended" gives us a somewhat coded account of community and offers reasons why this poet must find it dissatisfying. Another poem in the volume, "Clouds," will deal more severely with the need to break away, artistically speaking, from even the most nourishing community. "Soonest Mended" does not quite enact such a break, turning its gentler scrutiny on the poignant inability of any enclave whatsoever to satisfy the desire for true speech. This pathos comes through in a key passage where Ashbery sets the sign of disillusionment against the undeniably sweet faces of the others:

> This is what you wanted to hear, so why
> Did you think of listening to something else? We are all talkers
> It is true, but underneath the talk lies
> The moving and not wanting to be moved, the loose
> Meaning, untidy and simple like a threshing floor.

The powerful enjambment at the end of the third line in this quotation expresses all of Ashbery's ambivalence. "Underneath the talk lies"—so he might wish to leave it, until a softening sets in and he admits that beneath the deceit of social "talk" there hides the shifting forms of desire. The last line in this passage echoes the muse/mother's reprimand in "The Task"—"Just look at the filth you've made"—and here, too, the scatterings wait to be gathered into meaning. This vision of the others, the desired but not "extinct" community, will never fully betray or renounce the spirit of that time and place. It is enough to point, once, to the inevitable wounds that arise when we give and take in mere "talk." About this (least said), soonest mended.

Beyond conversation and beneath the colloquial texture of the poem lies the deep meaning of poetic language:

> Night after night this message returns, repeated
> In the flickering bulbs of the sky, raised past us, taken away
>   from us,
> Yet ours over and over until the end that is past truth,

The being of our sentences, in the climate that fostered them,
Not ours to own, like a book, but to be with, and sometimes
To be without, alone and desperate.

This is the credo that holds the haphazard aesthetic course together, and it is a credo Ashbery is willing to share. He does not astonish the others as he did in "Parergon." In fact, "Soonest Mended" ends with several attempts to register halting progress, so unlike the streaming movement at the close of "Parergon," as though Ashbery were trying to blend defeat with triumph. Does this, in the context of the poem, amount to a version of survivor guilt? Thus, the visionary moment becomes a "hard dole," "action" turns to uncertainty, preparation is "careless." And yet no degree of restraint can fully quell the sense of triumph and power attendant upon recovering the spot of origin at the poem's close. "That day so long ago," the day of poetic inauguration, does not belong to the time frame of memory. It belongs to a greater sequence. To understand the resonances of such a "day" it would help to look at the preceding poem in *The Double Dream*, "Plainness in Diversity." This lesser-known poem abbreviates the course traveled by "Soonest Mended" but moves in a remarkably similar direction. Once again it is the emptiness of "talk" that brings the truth home to the poetic quester; his place is elsewhere:

Silly girls your heads full of boys
There is a last sample of talk on the outer side
Your stand at last lifts to dumb evening
It is reflected in the steep blue sides of the crater,
So much water shall wash over these our breaths
Yet shall remain unwashed at the end. The fine
Branches of the fir tree catch at it, ebbing.
Not on our planet is the destiny
That can make you one.
To be placed on the side of some mountain
Is the truer story.

The second stanza continues to construct an outline of the journey myth, as it uses "the sagas" to discover a fitting point of origin and a worthy end to the quest:

There is so much they must say, and it is important
About all the swimming motions, and the way the hands
Came up out of the ocean with original fronds,
The famous arrow, the girls who came at dawn
To pay a visit to the young child, and how, when he grew up
　　to be a man
The same restive ceremony replaced the limited years
　　between,
Only now he was old, and forced to begin the journey to the
　　stars.

"Plainness in Diversity" locates us in myth more firmly than "Soonest Mended" chooses to do; but the gesture of starting out with which the latter concludes is also, surely, a version of heroism.

> —Charles Berger, "Vision in the Form of a Task: *The Double Dream of Spring*," *Beyond Amazement*, ed. David Lehman (Ithaca: Cornell University Press, 1980): 179–185.

JOHN HOLLANDER ON WINNOWING FRUIT FROM CHAFF

[John Hollander is the A. Bartlett Giamatti Professor of English at Yale and a Chancellor of the Academy of American Poets. His many honors include the Bollingen Prize in Poetry and a MacArthur Foundation Fellowship. In the following extract, Hollander explains how the poem defines meaning as the act of defining meaning.]

It is a poem not overheard, but one which more dangerously responds to the request for a word at a time of disaster—a quarrel, a dish dropped and broken, both perhaps amid the barely heard sounds of distant, rotten warfare. The very title of John Ashbery's "Soonest Mended" is half the proverb ("Least said, soonest mended") that it tries with self-descriptive *triage* to follow. It seems aware that we risk more, imaginatively, by speaking when we are spoken to than by merely being out of turn. Ashbery's opening flat, public diction, a pitch of the quotidian to which he frequently tunes on setting out, is in this poem immediately rescued—in the absence of Pegasus, in the loss even of the hippogriff of romance who replaced him—by the flapping wings of outlandish allusion. And thereby he takes seriously his three improbable opening clichés and is off on his poem in lieu of an apology:

> Barely tolerated, living on the margin
> In our technological society, we were always having to be rescued
> On the brink of destruction, like heroines in *Orlando Furioso*
> Before it was time to start all over again.
> There would be thunder in the bushes, a rustling of coils,
> And Angelica, in the Ingres painting, was considering
> The colorful but small monster near her toe, as though
>   wondering whether forgetting
> Might not in the end be the only solution.

Allusion—here, to Ariosto—and secondary allusion (to a problematic illustration of Ariosto, itself poised on the margins of silliness) have a strange power that keep for the user as much as they give. One of Ingres's studies for the Ruggiero and Angelica painting (at the Fogg Museum) is labeled "Perseus and Andromeda," the foreshadowing types of Ariosto's pair. But for the modern poet, the later figures are the fallen ones; and the losses are incurred in moving from myth to romance to gooey illustration to the contemporary moment of remembering all this in a time of need. This much the poet keeps for himself; what he gives us are the limits to the possibility of rescue. But forgetting, even in the presence of the toe of a muse imprisoned in academic painting's *fini*, is not only not the only solution: it is impossible. Even those of us who require wisdom seek after a sign. What next for Ashbery?

> And then there always came a time when
> Happy Hooligan in his rusted green automobile
> Came plowing down the course, just to make sure everything was O.K.,
> Only by that time we were in another chapter and confused
> About how to receive this latest piece of information.
> *Was* it information?

The hero astride the flying hippogriff or popping out of the rusted green automobile: unlike the "pagan in a varnished car" which Wallace Stevens had denied could descend into our lives as a capable fiction, the Imagination's rescuers dart in and out of the chapters of our daily story without the fanfare even of the certainty of their arrivals. This is the residue in major American poetry of the Wordsworthian view that redemptive vision will be there, when it is to be there at all, in the light of our ordinariness. The answer to Ashbery's question is that it was information, but could be authenticated only by having been able to elicit our doubt.

> *Was* it information? Weren't we rather acting this out
> For someone else's benefit, thoughts in a mind
> With room enough and to spare for our little problems (so
>   they began to seem).
> Our daily quandary about food and the rent and bills to be paid?

That daily quandary is the high noon of our usual attention, the state that W. H. Auden, whose language is indeed suggested in that last line, invoked as "the time being." It is not that succession of days from which we are, or desire, to be rescued; at the beginning of his great later poem, "Grand Galop," Ashbery makes clear that it is both *through* such a realm, as through an allegorical surrounding region, and by means of it, that the force of what we know can become the possible joy of what we do. At the beginning of a great walk through urban dreck which yields him as many seeds of light as ever glinted out at Henry Vaughan strolling through the West Country, Ashbery's vision of desiccated spring can lead him to the horrendous sequence of days in which poetic language need only name in order to act: "The weigela," he says,

> ... does its dusty thing
> In the fire-hammered air. And garbage cans are heaved against
> The railing as the tulips yawn and crack open and fall apart.
> And today is Monday. Today's lunch is: Spanish omelet,
>   lettuce and tomato salad,

> Jello, milk and cookies. Tomorrow's: sloppy joe on bun,
> Scalloped corn, stewed tomatoes, rice pudding and milk ...

(not an ecstatic Whitmanian catalogue, but more like a recital by W. C. Fields, trying to incapacitate further an already nauseated bank examiner). It is through, not from, the time of the dreadful lunches that our spirits are to pass, perhaps out into sunlight.—Or, at any rate, in "Soonest Mended,"

> To reduce all this to a small variant,
> To step free at last, minuscule on the gigantic plateau—
> This was our ambition: to be small and clear and free.

In an almost cinematic movement, the poem zooms away from this innuendo of sublimity; and the next strophe of the poem (although unmarked as such typographically) acknowledges its turn away from vision with an allusive touch of older tunes in its diction. Although with a Stevensian exclamation of "Pardie!" as unavailable to him now as a Horatian "Eheu!", the poet must minimize his wail, and move immediately to a confrontation with the difficulty of making poetic arrangements in a late time:

> Alas, the summer's energy wanes quickly,
> A moment and it is gone. And no longer
> May we make the necessary arrangements, simple as they are.

We want to ask, "But how simple *are* they?" What Ashbery elsewhere calls "Using what Wyatt and Surrey left around, / Took up and put down again / Like so much gorgeous raw material," is, after all, simple like the arrangements of the daily quandary from which poetry so differs and yet for which it stands. What is never simple is doing what we have to do at the time, at this time, whenever it is. How can fictions even less than supreme be of any importance now? How can poetry mirror what Shelley calls "the gigantic shadows which futurity casts upon the present" when the covering shade of the past makes such mirrored shadows almost unreadable? Ashbery's answer starts out with a terrifying acknowledgment of the ancestry of all our rhetorical and visionary reticence, and then moves into the central passage of the first half of the poem:

Our star was brighter perhaps when it had water in it.
Now there is no question even of that, but only
Of holding on to the hard earth so as not to get thrown off,
With an occasional dream, a vision: a robin flies across
The upper corner of the window, you brush your hair away
And cannot quite see, or a wound will flash
Against the sweet faces of the others, something like:
This is what you wanted to hear, so why
Did you think of listening to something else? We are all talkers
It is true, but underneath the talk lies
The moving and not wanting to be moved, the loose
Meaning, untidy and simple like a threshing floor.

This "meaning," its own chaff and fruit unwinnowed yet, is not only the meaning of our talk, our poems, our representations to each other of our lives, neat and complex as such deep structures have been held to be. It is more significantly the messy meaning of the word "meaning," the meaning of life. It is as if the poem had come upon its own central concern at the thirty-sixth of its seventy-one lines: Ashbery's resolved major theme of Getting On With It.

In "Soonest Mended" the theme manifests itself in its discovery that significances, moralizations, intentions—all the untidinesses of meaning—reach out from talking to what is talked about. Specifically, in the middle of the poem, the postmeridional time in the history of poetry, in the very chronicle of imaginings, resolves itself into the time of middle age. This is a poem of being forty-two or forty-three; what one had set out upon, whether or not in response to some vocation, twenty-five years or so earlier, will have been arrived at only in a surprising way. It is not only that the time of heroic rescues is over and that one finds oneself, in middle age, in America, awakening to the condition in which all the available heroisms are part of the predicament rather than the means of its dissolution. One discovers that acts of consciousness can be great acts as well:

These then were some hazards of the course,
Yet though we knew the course *was* hazards and nothing else
It was still a shock when, almost a quarter of a century later,
The clarity of the rules dawned on you for the first time.

They were the players, and we who had struggled at the game
Were merely spectators, though subject to its vicissitudes
And moving with it out of the tearful stadium, borne on
    shoulders, at last.

What kind of action is it, then, to try to grasp the meaning of what had been overflowing with possible significances? All our modern kind of poetic knowledge, all of the ways in which, from the major romantics on, we could possibly be instructed by our moments of vision as to how to live in between them, preclude the possibility of direct answers to such questions. The landscape or scene which is moralized by the very asking of the question, rather than, in the older poetry, an ultimately anagogic formula, returns in some hardened or reduced form as if in answer to the questioning. In Ashbery's poem, "the end that is past truth, / The being of our sentences, in the climate that fostered them" brings together our lives, what we have said of them, what we have—in both senses of the word—made of them. It is not only that men say things because they know they have been sentenced to death: what we say makes up our life sentences. What we could call "the poem of our lives" is at once the poem about our lives and the poem that is the individual life itself. What then, Ashbery goes on to ask, of the early poem when we awaken to our own request for a prose paraphrase? There is something scary about either refusing the request or trying to meet it; in any event, the early life affronts abstraction:

                These were moments, years,
Solid with reality, faces, namable events, kisses, heroic acts,
But like the friendly beginning of a geometrical progression
Not too reassuring, as though meaning could be cast aside some day
When it had been outgrown. Better, you said, to stay cowering
Like this in the early lessons, since the promise of learning
Is a delusion, and I agreed, adding that
Tomorrow would alter the sense of what had already been learned ...

"and," Ashbery continues, "probably thinking not to grow up / Is the brightest kind of maturity for us, right now at any rate."

The difference between "thinking not to grow up" and

pretending not to have done so is, in a way, the difference between a trivial, reductive reading of Ashbery's lines and the full—and, I hope that I have been suggesting, fully moral—one. Politically speaking, American visions of maturity—particularly during the nineteen-sixties and -seventies—should drive the good man screaming to the cradle. The businessman, the governor, and the soldier, they who represented the potent maturity of being all "balls" and, alternatively, the uncooperating stud who represented the potent maturity of being all cock-these maintained a cloven fiction of manliness, of being grown-up in America, that has always existed, but which the tasks and injunctions of our earlier history put to active use. Poetically speaking, this is the problem of how to get better, how to go on in any art without merely replicating what one can do well, without producing forgeries of one's earlier genuine work. In our losses, in our sense of time promised and time past slipping away from us, we American artists cannot say with Wordsworth in his *Elegiac Stanzas* "I have submitted to a new control"; instead, we move toward a subsequent messiness which we hope will redeem us from our successes.

For Ashbery in this poem, the dilemma about what to do with our beginnings resolves in the very act of contemplating ourselves as we are now. The astonishment at the realization of having arrived makes for a pause, but not a lack of motion. Life and art come together again in the lesson to be learned: our poems must get better, and we must all keep going. "And you see," he continues,

> ... both of us were right, though nothing
> Has somehow come to nothing; the avatars
> Of our conforming to the rules and living
> Around the home have made—well, in a sense, "good citizens" of us,
> Brushing the teeth and all that, and learning to accept
> The charity of the hard moments as they are doled out ...

Ashbery's continuous clarity makes us overlook the way his poetic surface is occasionally so beautifully wrought—I am thinking here of the precise and powerful definite article in "living / Around the home" (just "home" would give a sense of "hanging around," while "the home" makes it a purposive center of life). Similarly, "brushing the teeth" seems a powerful and delicate alteration of the more Audenesque "our teeth," the combined "our" of prayer, the editorial, and the nursery. If we think of the "hard moments"—difficult, windowless, durable in the memory—as being those of Ashbery's hard poem, we can understand how, in that poem, they are the moments of life itself. The difficulties of, and in, our fictions recapitulate those of the rest of our lives. Ashbery's final, firm, almost measured lines conclude his poem with a substitute for the traditional openings—out of landscape, or closings-in of shadows, which the visionary lyric in English derived from Virgil's eclogues and made its own. The conclusion they draw, in an expository sense, is a substitute for heroic resolution, or reductive hope, or a tired, tragic commitment to keeping the inner beasts of disorder chained up as well as one can. The poem has acknowledged its response to the truth about lives to be "a kind of fence-sitting / Raised to the level of an esthetic ideal"; how can it draw itself to a close? Ashbery's measured appositives to "not being sure" hide their startling revisions of the ordinary language—even the cliché—of resolution almost until they have themselves drifted by:

> For this is action, this is not being sure, this careless
> Preparing, sowing seeds crooked in the furrow,
> Making ready to forget, and always coming back
> To the mooring of starting out, that day so long ago.

One of these revisions accounts for the deep resonance of "making ready to forget"—not making ready to forget life, and to be forgotten, in death, making ready to die; but in fact, making ready to live and to be living. The other brings about the apparent oxymoron of "the mooring of starting out." Not only is there an alteration of the expected "the morning of starting out." There is also rather a matter of condensation than contradiction; at a more purely Stevensian rhetorical moment in his work, Ashbery might have glossed his image more by playing about with the consequences of the metaphor. "It is not that starting out on artistic and, indeed, generally human courses of wisdom is a matter of cutting loose from moorings—no complex consciousness could without the crudest of ironies utter 'I'm adrift, I'm adrift' in avowal of its uncertainty. It is only that the starting out itself, the vocation, the initiation of serious life, is all that we can be, or authentically *be said in a real poem to be*, moored to. The trope of moorings and the sea voyage of life can only apply when troped itself." Something like this, in dialectic but certainly not in language, might have provided a passage of an earlier style of American poetic meditation. The very difficulty of this kind of poetry is the difficulty of having it be true of our lives, of having its art unfold in wisdom.

—John Hollander, "A Poetry of Restitution." *Yale Review* 70, no. 2 (Winter, 1981): 171–178

HAROLD BLOOM ON THE TWICE-BORN LIFE

[Harold Bloom is Sterling Professor of the Humanities at Yale University and Henry W. and Albert A. Berg Professor of English at the New York University Graduate School. He is the author of over 20 books, including *The Western Canon* and *How to Read and Why*, and the editor of dozens more. In this extract, Bloom draws on aspects of his theory of the anxiety of influence to contextualize both the poem and Ashbery's career as a whole.]

Though the leap in manner between *Rivers and Mountains* and *The Double Dream of Spring* is less prodigious than the gap between *The Tennis Court Oath* and *Rivers and Mountains*, there is a more crucial change in the later transition. Ashbery at last says farewell to ellipsis, a farewell confirmed by *Three Poems*, which relies upon "putting it all in," indeed upon the discursiveness of a still-demanding prose. The abandonment of Ashbery's rhetorical evasiveness is a self-curtailment on his part, a purgation that imparts simplicity through intensity, but at the price of returning him to the rhetorical world of Stevens and of the American tradition that led to Stevens. It is rather as if Browning had gone from his grotesque power backwards to the

Shelleyan phase of his work. Perhaps Browning should have, since his last decades were mostly barren. As a strong poet, Ashbery has matured almost as slowly as his master Stevens did, though unlike Stevens he has matured in public. Even as Stevens provoked a critical nonsense, only now vanishing, of somehow being a French poet writing in English, so Ashbery still provokes such nonsense. Both are massive sufferers from the anxiety-of-influence, and both developed only when they directly engaged their American precursors. In Ashbery, the struggle with influence, though more open, is also more difficult, since Ashbery desperately engages also the demon of discursiveness, as Hart Crane differently did (for the last stand of Crane's mode, see the one superb volume of Alvin Feinman, *Preambles And Other Poems*, 1964). This hopeless engagement, endemic in all Western poetries in our century, is a generalized variety of the melancholy of poetic influence. It is not problematic form, nor repressed allusiveness, nor recondite matter, that makes much modern verse difficult. Nor, except rarely, is it conceptual profundity, or sustained mythical invention. Ellipsis, the art of omission, almost always a central device in poetry, has been abused into the dominant element rhetorically of our time. Yet no modern poet has employed it so effectively as Dickinson did, probably because for her it was a deep symptom of everything else that belonged to the male tradition that she was leaving out. I cannot involve myself here in the whole argument that I have set forth in a little book, *The Anxiety of Influence: A Theory of Poetry* (1973; see the discussion of Ashbery in the section called "*Apophrades*: or the Return of the Dead"), but I cite it as presenting evidence for the judgment that influence becomes progressively more of a burden for poets from the Enlightenment to this moment. Poets, defending poetry, are adept at idealizing their relation to one another, and the magical Idealists among critics have followed them in this saving self-deception. Here is Northrop Frye, greatest of the idealizers:

Once the artist thinks in terms of influence rather than of clarity of form, the effort of the imagination becomes an effort of will, and art is perverted into tyranny, the application of the principle of magic or mysterious compulsion to society.

Against this I cite Coleridge's remark that the power of originating is the will, our means of escaping from nature or repetition-compulsion, and I add that no one needs to pervert art in this respect, since the Post-Enlightenment poetic imagination is necessarily quite perverse enough in the perpetual battle against influence. Wordsworth is a misinterpretation of Milton (as is Blake), Shelley is a misinterpretation of Wordsworth, Browning and Yeats *are* misinterpretations of Shelley. Or, in the native strain, Whitman perverts or twists askew Emerson, Stevens is guilty of misprision towards both, and Ashbery attempts a profound and beautiful misinterpretation of all his precursors, *in his own best poetry*. What the elliptical mode truly seeks to omit is the overt continuity with ancestors, and the mysterious compulsion operative here is a displacement of what Freud charmingly called "the family romance."

Ashbery's own family romance hovers uneasily in all-but-repressed memories of childhood; his family-romance-as-poet attains a momentarily happy resolution in *The Double Dream of Spring*, but returns darkly in *Three Poems*. Ashbery is a splendid instance of the redemptive aspect of influence-anxiety, for his best work shows how the relation to the precursor is humanized into the greater themes of all human influence-relations, which after all include lust, envy, sexual jealousy, the horror of families, friendship, and the poet's reciprocal relation to his contemporaries, ultimately to all of his readers.

I begin again, after this anxious digression, with "Soonest Mended," and begin also the litany of praise and advocacy, of what Pater called "appreciation," that the later work of Ashbery inspires in me. The promise of *Some Trees* was a long time realizing itself, but the realization came, and Ashbery is now something close to a great poet. It is inconvenient to quote all of "Soonest Mended," but I will discuss it as though my reader is staring at pages 17 through 19 of *The Double Dream of Spring*. The poem speaks for the artistic life of Ashbery's generation, but more for the general sense of awakening to the haphazardness and danger of one's marginal situation in early middle age:

> *To step free at last, minuscule on the gigantic plateau—*
> *This was our ambition: to be small and clear and free.*

Alas, the summer's energy wanes quickly,
A moment and it is gone. And no longer
May we make the necessary arrangements, simple as they are.
Our star was brighter perhaps when it had water in it.
Now there is no question even of that, but only
Of holding on to the hard earth so as not to get thrown off,
With an occasional dream, a vision ...

Dr. Johnson, still the most useful critic in the language, taught us to value highly any original expression of common or universal experience. "Has he any fresh matter to disclose?" is the question Johnson would have us ask of any new poet whose work seems to demand our deep consideration. The Ashbery of his two most recent volumes passes this test triumphantly. "Soonest Mended," from its rightly proverbial title through every line of its evenly distributed rumination, examines freshly that bafflement of the twice-born life that has been a major theme from Rousseau and Wordsworth to Flaubert and Stevens. This is the sense of awakening, past the middle of the journey, to the truth that: "*they* were the players, and we who had struggled at the game / Were merely spectators ..." Uniquely, Ashbery's contribution is the wisdom of a wiser passivity:

... learning to accept
The charity of the hard moments as they are doled out,
For this is action, this not being sure, this careless
Preparing, sowing the seeds crooked in the furrow,
Making ready to forget, and always coming back
To the mooring of starting out, that day so long ago.

Action, Wordsworth said, was momentary, only a step or blow, but suffering was permanent, obscure, dark and shared the nature of infinity. Ashbery's action is Wordsworth's suffering; the way through to it, Ashbery says, is "a kind of fence-sitting / Raised to the level of an esthetic ideal." If time indeed is an emulsion, as this poem asserts, then wisdom is to find the mercy of eternity in the charity of the hard moments. Shelley, forgiving his precursors, said that they had been washed in the blood of the redeemer and mediator, time. Ashbery domesticates this fierce idealism; "conforming to the rules and living/Around the home" mediate his vision, and redemption is the indefinite extension of the learning process, even if the extension depends upon conscious fantasy. The achievement of "Soonest Mended" is to have told a reductive truth, yet to have raised it out of reductiveness by a persistence masked as the communal, an urgency made noble by art.

> —Harold Bloom, "The Charity of Hard Moments," *Modern Critical Views: John Ashbery* (New York: Chelsea House, 1985): 60–63.

VERNON SHETLEY ON ASHBERY'S FLOATING PRONOUNS

[Vernon Shetley is a Professor of English at Wesleyan University. In addition to his full-length study of the relationship between poet and audience in postwar American, from which the following is extracted, he is the author of numerous articles on poetry and film. In this extract, Shetley investigates how Ashbery's manipulation of pronouns undermines the New Criticism's "speaker-situation" model of interpretation.]

Poetry, Ashbery remarks in an interview, is "not a cottage industry in America but a college industry" (Sommer 299), and the New Criticism, perhaps inadvertently, did much to make that possible. One of the chief mechanisms by which it made modernist difficulty teachable was the explicitly dramatistic mode of reading it encouraged, in which the key interpretive terms became *speaker* and *situation*. This principle is spelled out in the introduction to Cleanth Brooks and Robert Penn Warren's widely used textbook, *Understanding Poetry*:

> All poetry, including even short lyrics or descriptive pieces ..., involves a dramatic organization. This is clear when we reflect that every poem implies a speaker of the poem, either the poet writing in his own person or someone into whose mouth the poem is put, and that the poem represents the reaction of such a person to a situation, a scene, or an idea. In reading poetry it is

well to remember this dramatic aspect and to be sure that one sees the part it plays in any given poem. [23]

Reading according to the master terms *speaker* and *situation* helped smooth over the jagged and problematic discontinuities of much modernist writing, enabling apparent breakdowns in coherence to be recoded as dramatic representations securely under the control of the poet's formal impulse. So, in their discussion of T. S. Eliot's "The Love Song of J. Alfred Prufrock," Brooks and Warren appeal to the paradigm of speaker and situation to salvage a notion of the poem's unity from its own disjunctions: "The transitions here appear, at first glance ... violent. This apparent violence disappears, however, as soon as we realize that the relations between the various scenes, ideas, and observations in the poem are determined by a kind of flow of associations which are really based on the fact that they develop and illustrate the fundamental character and situation of Prufrock" (591). The violent and apparently arbitrary transitions that characterize modernist style are here brought back within the confines of the New Critical dictum of organic unity. If, as Brooks and Warren remark, the poem's "primary difficulty for the reader is the apparent lack of logical transitions" (595), New Critical reading accommodates poem to reader by filling in that absence, thus pacifying the threatening "violence" of the poem. *Speaker* and *situation*, then, become important critical tools in producing a "college industry" of modernism, and it is on the reading practices engendered by these categories that Ashbery's resistance to the institutionalization of the avant-garde focuses.

Ashbery's manipulation of pronouns plays a leading role in his dismantling of the speaker–situation model. Personal pronouns shift and blur, and impersonals and relatives such as *it* and *this* float through the poems detached from any easily ascertained referent. "I" often gives way without warning to "you" or "them," or one in a series of similar pronouns will suddenly seem to have a different antecedent from its companions. Ashbery remarks about this effect: "I guess I don't have a very strong sense of my own identity and I find it very easy to move from one person in the sense of a pronoun to another" (*NYQ* 25). The notion of persona or mask was a critical element in modernist poetics and the criticism it fostered; the persona posited an ironic distance between poet and speaker, through which the expressive impulse could be transformed into the impersonality that was so much a New Critical desideratum. Ashbery proposes, however, not ironic distance but an undecidable blurring or wavering, a confusion antithetical to the New Critical notion of speaker. Similarly, the broad gestures of Ashbery's vaguely defined impersonal and relative pronouns point to what might rather be called a *condition* than a *situation* conceived in the dramatistic terms of the New Criticism. Such gestures at once insist on the importance of the contexts they suggest and leave those contexts tantalizingly obscure, asking the reader to fill in the blanks opened in the poem. In doing so, the pronouns produce not the ironically distanced situations favored by New Critical reading but a wavering and indeterminate suggestion of identity between the contexts of poet, poem, and reader.

Donald Davie's remarks on wandering pronoun reference in Shelley's verse may help us imagine the reaction of a reader imbued with New Critical values to Ashbery's free treatment of pronouns. Citing a stanza from Shelley's "The Cloud," Davie notes that the passage "comes to grief on the loose use of a personal pronoun" (136), then goes on to lament that "this looseness occurs time and again." After quoting this further passage from the poem,

> The stars peep behind her and peer;
> And I laugh to see them whirl and flee,
> Like a swarm of golden bees,
> When I widen the rent in my wind-built tent,
> Till the calm rivers, lakes, and seas,
> Like strips of the sky fallen through me on high,
> Are paved with the moon and these.

he exclaims that "the grotesque 'and these' is an affront to all prosaic discipline." Affronts to discipline such as the lapses Davie identifies in Shelley generally brought down charges of "muddle" or "fuzziness"—perhaps the two most damning terms in the New Critical lexicon. Ashbery, however, has chosen to write as if entirely unafraid of provoking such charges; he employs pronouns in just the way Davie here protests.

"Soonest Mended" offers an excellent example of the deliberately vague handling of pronoun reference that characterizes Ashbery's style:

> Barely tolerated, living on the margin
> In our technological society, we were always having to be
>   rescued
> On the brink of destruction, like heroines in *Orlando Furioso*
> Before it was time to start all over again.
> There would be thunder in the bushes, a rustling of coils,
> And Angelica, in the Ingres painting, was considering
> The colorful but small monster near her toe, as though
>   wondering whether forgetting
> The whole thing might not, in the end, be the only solution.
> And then there always came a time when
> Happy Hooligan in his rusted green automobile
> Came plowing down the course, just to make sure everything
>   was O.K.,
> Only by that time we were in another chapter and confused
> About how to receive this latest piece of information.
> *Was* it information? Weren't we rather acting this out
> For someone else's benefit, thoughts in a mind
> With room enough and to spare for our little problems (so
>   they began to seem),
> Our daily quandary about food and the rent and bills
>   to be paid?
> To reduce all this to a small variant,
> To step free at last, minuscule on the gigantic plateau—
> This was our ambition: to be small and clear and free.
> [*DDS* 17]

"The whole thing ... everything ... this ... all this": the passage is linked together by a chain of gestures toward some large, encompassing whole that conditions the utterance of the poem, furnishes its context, at the same time that this context seems continually to shift, one frame to replace another. The simile in the first sentence exfoliates into a whole scenario (bounded by the frame of "the Ingres painting"), which is in turn quickly swept away, as if the poem too were "forgetting the whole thing." The frame then shifts from gilt to newsprint with the arrival of Happy Hooligan, so it seems likely that "everything" here is rather different from "the whole thing" put aside in the previous sentence, while with the return of the "we" the cartoon figure becomes enclosed within a "chapter" (of our lives? of a serial?), suddenly telescoped from a space shared with us to the flatness of the page. And yet the same operation is immediately performed, if only provisionally, upon the "we" of the passage, who are placed within a further expanded framework, becoming "thoughts in a mind." Even the definite article comes into play as a means of ambiguation. Terming it *the* gigantic plateau" implies the reader's familiarity with the object, yet the poem does nothing to place the reference; it becomes one more situation or frame of reference that dissolves before it has stabilized.

The fluid transformations of situation in the poem are matched by its similar play with the speaking subject. The opening lines apparently address a specific individual or group that shares a particular experience with the poet; by the end of the passage quoted above, however, it seems clear that the application of this "we" has become generalized to include the poem's audience, all those who share the desire to "step free." Yet suddenly a "you" enters the poem, a "you" that seems sharply delineated and specific:

> a robin flies across
> The upper corner of the window, you brush your hair away
> And cannot quite see, or a wound will flash
> Against the sweet faces of the others, something like:
> This is what you wanted to hear, so why
> Did you think of listening to something else?
> [*DDS* 18]

As it continues, the poem seems to oscillate between according the "you" a separate identity and folding it back into the "we":

> These then were some hazards of the course,
> Yet though we knew the course *was* hazards and nothing else
> It was still a shock when, almost a quarter of a century later,

The clarity of the rules dawned on you for the first time.
They were the players, and we who had struggled at the game
Were merely spectators, though subject to its vicissitudes
And moving with it out of the tearful stadium, borne on
    shoulders, at last.
[*DDS* 18]

A typically Ashberyan play with pronoun reference in this passage sets up a further play of distance and proximity between "we" and "they." Tracing back, one finds that the "it" in the final line refers to "the game"; one usually thinks of a game's being over when players and spectators leave the stadium, but here the game itself is what moves out of the stadium, as if the stadium were simply one more of the framing structures that dissolve or give way in the course of the poem, leaving the "we" in a position similar to the "players" to which it had earlier been opposed. As when the poet imagines "us" as "thoughts in a mind," this passage figures the position of marginality posited in the poem's opening as both attractive and disturbing. Being out of the game provokes anxiety while at the same time opening a potentially liberating distance from the "struggle."

The play between the elements that inhabit the poem's "we" receives a further turn as "I" and "you" engage in a moment of dialogue:

                  Better, you said, to stay cowering
Like this in the early lessons, since the promise of learning
Is a delusion, and I agreed, adding that
Tomorrow would alter the sense of what had already been
    learned,
That the learning process is extended in this way, so that from
    this standpoint
None of us ever graduates from college,
For time is an emulsion, and probably thinking not to grow up
Is the brightest kind of maturity for us, right now at any rate.
[*DDS* 18–19]

This dialogue, however, diminishes rather than confirms the distinction between these two speakers, as if this "you" and "I" were akin to Prufrock's, a figure for some division within the self. The final appearances of the first-person plural seem deliberately to expand and contract at once its range of reference:

> And you see, both of us were right, though nothing
> Has somehow come to nothing; the avatars
> Of our conforming to the rules and living
> Around the home have made—well, in a sense, "good
>   citizens" of us,
> Brushing the teeth and all that, and learning to accept
> The charity of the hard moments as they are doled out,
> For this is action, this not being sure, this careless
> Preparing, sowing the seeds crooked in the furrow,
> Making ready to forget, and always coming back
> To the mooring of starting out, that day so long ago.
> [*DDS* 19]

"Both of us" narrows the pronoun to "I" and "you," while the final passage seems once again to open out to include the poem's readers, all those who share the circumstances of their lives with the poet. A similar expansion of reference takes place in "Prufrock" as the "we" introduced in the final lines seems to exceed the "you and I" of the opening, which denominates only Prufrock himself. Prufrock, however, remains defined by his distance from the "human" society around him, while in Ashbery's poem, in the last of its many revisions and reframings, the lines of demarcation blur between this "we" and the "society" in opposition to which it is defined in the poem's opening. Prufrock's final "we" functions as if the poem had suddenly reached out to take you with it as it goes down gasping, while "Soonest Mended" shuttles fluidly among that pronoun's various possibilities. "Prufrock" reaches out of the frame it has constructed, but only to drag the reader in, while "Soonest Mended" continually puts into question what is inside and what is outside the frame. The marginalized poet has become a "good citizen," but only "in a sense."

> —Vernon Shetley, *After the Death of Poetry: Poet and Audience in Contemporary America* (Durham: Duke University Press, 1993): 110–116.

"Self-Portrait in a Convex Mirror"

As in "Soonest Mended," the immediacy of the opening lines of "Self-Portrait" suggests an inquiry or dialogue well underway. In addition to brilliantly describing the titular painting, these lines, and quite a few more within the poem, also serve as apt descriptions of the poem itself. "As Parmigianino did it, the right hand / Bigger than the head / thrust at the viewer / And swerving easily away, as though to protect / What it advertises." Ashbery creates an implicit dichotomy between what is created ("hand") and what is thought ("head"). Whether the former can truly represent the latter, and what that representation reveals, are the questions, variously formulated, that the poem sets out to explore.

But just in case readers are unfamiliar with the small, halved wooden ball on which the 16th-century Mannerist painter Francesco Parmigianino "set himself / With great art to copy" his reflection in a convex mirror, Ashbery includes a concise introduction in the words of prototypical art historian Giorgio Vasari. The quote simultaneously raises Parmigianino's ante with a reflection thrice removed (the poem, of course, continues this infinite progression) and satirizes the style and implicit goal of art criticism, which is to lend the appearance of objective reality to one's own personal interpretation: "The glass chose to reflect only what he saw."

The metaphor of two mirrors proximately positioned to create a series of embedded reflections was not a new one when Ashbery sat down, sometime between 1973 and 1974, to write "Self-Portrait." Nor was the theory that a meditation on this phenomenon might reveal something profound about the limitations or potential of art and the human mind. A variation on the theme occurs as early as Plato's *Timaeus* and writers, philosophers, and painters have been toying with the idea ever since. Few, if any, however, can match Ashbery's replication of the double mirror's aesthetic effects—the disorienting confusion of illusory depths, the paradoxical sense of entrapment within infinite space, or the way multifarious perspectives render a subject "in a recurring wave / Of arrival." But then again, Ashbery also had the fortune to be writing at a historical moment uniquely suited to such a meditation. Deconstructionism, Semiotics, and modern psychoanalytic theory had saturated the cultural landscape with such concepts as Self vs. Other, Signifier vs. Signified, Real vs. Simulacrum, to the point where Ashbery had no need to reference them directly. Veritable proof that he wrote the right poem at the right time can be found in the fact that, after its publication, Ashbery literally entered the Canon overnight by winning the "triple crown" of modern American literature: the Pulitzer Prize, the National Book Award, and the National Book Critics Circle Award.

Historical context is hardly enough to explain the poem's brilliance, however, which lies in its ability to anticipate and self-reflexively critique each of its digressions with an economy of language and metaphor that matches the technical mastery of the painting. "The soul establishes itself. / But how far can it swim out through the eyes / And still return safely to its nest?" As the phrases begin to take on double and triple layers of resonance, it quickly dawns on the reader that Ashbery isn't just talking about Parmigianino's painting or his own unique brand of poetry, but the disconnect between the static nature of art and language and the ever-fluctuating dynamics of consciousness. "The words are only speculation / (From the Latin *speculum*, mirror): / They seek and cannot find the meaning of the music." In order to more accurately represent consciousness, Ashbery taps into a constant flow of ideas forever on the verge of re-formulation. He does so in six long stanzas or verse paragraphs that each contain their own interpretations and re-interpretations of the painting's aesthetic and philosophical implications. In lieu of a line-by-line reading, which would require a book of its own, I will now attempt to parse out the general progression of the poem's argument.

In section one, Ashbery begins with an appreciation of the painting's technique and the compelling paradox of its ability to simultaneously attract and repel the viewer's gaze. The more he thinks about this quality, though, and the more he notes the lifelessness of the rendering, the more he is convinced that it represents an entrapment of the painter's reflection and thus his soul. Ashbery's reaction to this revelation is one of the most memorable sections of the poem: "The secret is too plain. The pity of it smarts, / Makes hot tears spurt: that the soul is not a soul, / Has no secret, is small, and it fits / Its hollow perfectly: its room, our moment of attention."

Section two turns away momentarily from the painting and this disturbing interpretation (this "affirmation that doesn't affirm anything") to focus on Ashbery, as he sits "in the silence of the studio" and "considers / Lifting the pencil to [his own] self portrait." Remembering all the moments and memories "that became part of" him, Ashbery chafes at the notion that Parmigianino's aesthetic would "boil down" all those things that make him an individual and create "one / Uniform substance, a magma of interiors."

Having considered and refused the painting's example, Ashbery is free in section three to engage in a more detached, broader inquiry. At first he decides that Parmagianino has been helpful after all—by employing such a mannered perspective, perhaps he reveals the bias inherent in all art, "a weak instrument though / Necessary." Moreover, that small aperture, that "one piece of surface" might be able to show us the way to true vision, "letting one ramble / Back home." Ashbery quickly rejects this reading, however. To accept such an impoverished view of art is to deprive humans of their inherent wealth, "leaving us / To awake and try to begin living in what / Has now become a slum." Unsurprisingly, Ashbery just as swiftly doubles back; perhaps that very impoverishing will motivate us to greater things. "We notice the holes the dreams left. Now their importance / If not their meaning is plain." Furthermore, we might not have any choice in the matter, so "Why be unhappy with this arrangement, since / Dreams prolong us as they are absorbed? / Something like living occurs, a movement / Out of the dream into its codification."

Section four finds Ashbery further probing this "something like living" to see if in its Otherness we can find our forgotten likeness: "you could be fooled for a moment / Before you realize the reflection / Isn't yours." Again this proves troubling, though, alright in concept, "except that the whole of me / Is seen to be supplanted by the strict / Otherness of the painter in his / Other room." The repetition of "other" here, reinforced by its capitalization, drives home the difference between the painting's circumscribed world and the "whole of" Ashbery's more fluid existence.

Section five again expands the poem's scope, breaking the painting's spell by revealing it as just one context within many: "Rome where Francesco / Was at work during the Sack…Vienna where the painting is today … New York / Where I am now." New artistic wonders, "a new preciosity" will inevitably supplant the painting in Ashbery's consciousness, an "unlikely / Challenger pounding on the gates of an amazed / Castle." In light of promised new wonders, Francesco's mute stare grows "stale as no answer / Or answers were forthcoming." And yet, Ashbery cannot fully break away; he wonders if maybe he has overlooked something. "It may be that another life is stocked there / In recesses no one knew of; that it, / Not we, are the change; that we are in fact it / If we could get back to it."

Section six subjects the poem that the painting has helped create to the same scrutiny, beginning the cycle all over again, and reaching a similar, but more textured, conclusion to the one arrived at in section three. Though art is a "weak instrument" with which we can never fully communicate the richness of our souls, we might as well use what we have because "this otherness, this / 'Not-being-us' is all there is to look at / In the mirror, though no one can say / How it came to be this way."

It should be noted that, although helpful in terms of comprehension, this breaking the poem down into constituent lines of reasoning is in some ways missing the point, as it reduces a holistic multivalence into an exercise in forensics. Ashbery once said, "What I like about music is its ability to be convincing, to carry an argument through successfully to the finish, though the terms of the argument remain unknown quantities." Fortunately, Ashbery's verse is musical enough to withstand paraphrase, regaining the feel of an "unknown quantity" on every reading.

As a final disclaimer, due to both space considerations and the resistance of some longer essays to cogent extraction, it was not possible to sample every insightful piece of writing on "Self-Portrait." As such, readers are encouraged to check to the bibliography for additional examples, particularly those by Charles Altieri and Robert Mueller.

"Self-Portrait in a Convex Mirror"

DAVID KALSTONE ON REVISIONS WITHIN AND WITHOUT

[David Kalstone, a Professor of English at Rutgers University until his death in 1986, was the author of several books, including *Becoming a Poet* and *Five Temperaments*. In the following extract, Kalstone examines the poem's tendency to revise its own interpretation of the painting, as well as actual revisions Ashbery made to the original text before its publication.]

"Self-Portrait" begins quietly, not overcommitted to its occasion, postponing full sentences, preferring phrases:

> As Parmigianino did it, the right hand
> Bigger than the head, thrust at the viewer
> And swerving easily away, as though to protect
> What it advertises. A few leaded panes, old beams,
> Fur, pleated muslin, a coral ring rung together
> In a movement supporting the face, which swims
> Toward and away like the hand
> Except that it is in repose. It is what is
> Sequestered.

A lot could be said about Ashbery's entrance into poems and his habit of tentative anchorage: "As on a festal day in early spring," "As One Put Drunk into the Packet Boat" (title: first line of Marvell's "Tom May's Death"). Such openings are reticent, similes taking on the identity of another occasion, another person—a sideways address to their subject or, in the case of "Self-Portrait," a way of dealing with temptation. The speaker in "Self-Portrait" appears to "happen" upon Parmigianino's painting as a solution to a problem pondered before the poem begins. At first glimpse the glass of art and the face in the portrait offer him just the right degree of self-disclosure and self-assertion, the right balance of living spirit and the haunting concentrated maneuvers of art. The judicious give-and-take appears to him: thrust and swerve; toward and away; protect and advertise. (This is, by the way, one of the best descriptive impressions of a painting I know.) That balanced satisfaction never returns. What at first comforts him, the face "in repose," prompts an unsettling fear: "It is what is / Sequestered." This is the first full sentence of the poem—brief, shocked and considered, after the glancing descriptive phrases. An earlier draft of the lines was weaker: "protected" rather than "sequestered" and the word placed unemphatically at the end of the line, as if some of the menace to be sensed in the finished portrait hadn't yet surfaced.

From then on the poem becomes, as Ashbery explains it in a crucial pun, "speculation / (From the Latin *speculum*, mirror)," Ashbery's glass rather than Francesco's. All questions of scientific reflection, capturing a real presence, turn instantly into the other kind of reflection: changeable, even fickle thought. The whole poem is a series of revisions prepared for in the opening lines, where in Parmigianino's receding portrait he imagines first that "the soul establishes itself," then that "the soul is a captive." Finally, from the portrait's mixture of "tenderness, amusement and regret":

> The secret is too plain. The pity of it smarts,
> Makes hot tears spurt: that the soul is not a soul,
> Has no secret, is small, and it fits
> Its hollow perfectly: its room, our moment of attention.

In an earlier draft of the poem it was not quite so clear why such strong feeling emerges:

> ... that the soul
> Has no secret, is small, though it fits
> Perfectly the space intended for it: its room, our attention.

Rewriting those lines Ashbery allowed more emphatic fears to surface. "The soul is not a soul." Acting on an earlier hint that Parmigianino's mirror chose to show an image "glazed, embalmed," Ashbery sees it in its hollow (overtones of burial) rather than in the neutral "space intended." "Our moment of attention" draws sparks between the glazed surface of the portrait and the poet's transient interest which awakens it, and places notions like the *soul* irredeemably in the eye of the beholder. When the poet looks at this ghostly double, alive in its mirroring appeal, the emerging fear comes across like Milly Theale's (*The Wings of the Dove*) in front of the Bronzino portrait resembling her, "dead, dead, dead."

Throughout "Self-Portrait in a Convex Mirror" the poet speaks to the portrait as in easy consultation with a familiar, but with an ever changing sense of whether he is addressing the image, trapped on its wooden globe, or addressing the free painter standing outside his creation, straining to capture a real presence, restraining the power to shatter what may become a prison: "Francesco, your hand is big enough / To wreck the sphere, ..." An explosion has been building from the start as Ashbery returns over and over, puzzled by that hand which the convex mirror shows "Bigger than the head, thrust at the viewer / And swerving easily away, as though to protect / What it advertises." At first that defensive posture in a work of art attracts him, an icon of mastery. But, a little later, feeling the portrait as "life englobed," he reads the hand differently:

> One would like to stick one's hand
> Out of the globe, but its dimension,
> What carries it, will not allow it.
> No doubt it is this, not the reflex
> To hide something, which makes the hand loom large
> As it retreats slightly.

The hand returns not in self-defense, but

> ... to fence in and shore up the face
> On which the effort of this condition reads
> Like a pinpoint of a smile, a spark.
> Or star one is not sure of having seen
> As darkness resumes.

Philosophic questions mount, but always apprehended through gestures, new expressions glimpsed as one stares at the painting—here a glint of self-mockery, as the painter absorbed with prowess finds himself trapped by his medium after all. "But your eyes proclaim / That everything is surface.... / There are no recesses in the room, only alcoves." The window admits light, but all sense of change is excluded, even "the weather, which in French is / *Le temps*, the word for time." The opening section of "Self-Portrait" winds down, the poet bemused but his poetry drained of the emotional concentration which had drawn him to the painting; a glance at the subject's hands sees them as symbolically placed, but inexpressive:

> The whole is stable within
> Instability, a globe like ours, resting
> On a pedestal of vacuum, a ping-pong hall
> Secure on its jet of water.
> And just as there are no words for the surface, that is,
> No words to say what it really is, that it is not
> Superficial but a visible core, then there is
> No way out of the problem of pathos vs. experience.
> You will stay on, restive, serene in
> Your gesture which is neither embrace nor warning
> But which holds something of both in pure
> Affirmation that doesn't affirm anything.

This is not Ashbery's final reading of the portrait's gesturing hand. But it launches a series of struggles with the past, with "art," with the notion of "surface," with the random demands of the present—struggles which are not only at the heart of this poem but a paradigm of Ashbery's work. Parmigianino's portrait has to compete with the furniture of the mind confronting it: the poet's day, memories, surroundings, ambitions, distractions. The solid spherical segment becomes confused, in the Wonderland of the mind, with other rounded images, toys of attention—a ping-pong ball on a jet of water, and then, at the start of the second section, "The balloon pops, the attention / Turns dully away." There is a rhythm to reading this poem, however wandering it may seem. We experience it as a series of contractions and expansions of interest in the painting, depending upon how much the poet is drawn to its powers of foreshortening and concentration, and alternately how cramped he feels breathing its air. The transitions between sections are marked as ease shifts in inner weather, opposed to the weatherless chamber of Parmigianino's portrait:

> The balloon pops, the attention
> Turns dully away.
>
> As I start to forget it
> It presents its stereotype again
>
> The shadow of the city injects its own
> Urgency:
>
> A breeze like the turning of a page
> Brings back your face.

The painting occurs to him at times as a ship: first, a "tiny, self-important ship / On the surface." In mysterious relation to it the enlarged hand in the distorted portrait seems "Like a dozing whale on the sea bottom." Threatening? Or a sign of throbbing vitality, an invisible part of its world? Later the portrait

> ... is an unfamiliar stereotype, the face
> Riding at anchor, issued from hazards, sown
> To accost others, "rather angel than man" (Vasari).

Toward the end of the poem, the ship sails in to confirm some sense of

> ... this otherness
> That gets included in the most ordinary
> Forms of daily activity, changing everything
> Slightly and profoundly, and tearing the matter
> Of creation, any creation, not just artistic creation
> Out of our hands, to install it on some monstrous, near
> Peak, too close to ignore, too far
> For one to, intervene? This otherness, this

"Not-being-us" is all there is to look at
In the mirror, though no one can say
How it came to he this way. A ship
Flying unknown colors has entered the harbor.

Self-important and tiny? Issued from hazards? Flying unknown
colors? Through contradictory senses of the ship, Ashbery
judges the portrait's relation to risk and adventure, to the
mysterious otherness of "arrival" in a completed work of art.

—David Kalstone, "'Self–Portrait in a Convex Mirror,'" *Five
Temperments* (Oxford: Oxford University Press, 1977): 176–181.

RICHARD STAMELMAN ON A NEW KIND OF EKPHRASIS

[Richard Stamelman is a Professor of Romance Languages
and Comparative Literature at Williams College. In
addition to articles on modern American and French poetry
and translations of Edmond Jabes and Yves Bonnefoy, he is
the author of *Lost Beyond Telling: Representations of Death and
Absence in Modern French Poetry*. In the following excerpt,
Stamelman explains how the poem circumvents the
typically arresting effect of ekphrasis and thus subverts
standard notions of artistic representation and temporal
immobility.]

As a rhetorical term *ekphrasis* denotes any vivid, self-contained,
autonomous description that is part of a longer discourse; it is
generally accepted, however, to refer to the written imitation of
a work of plastic art. The shield of Achilles as described by
Homer in Book XVIII of the *Iliad* as the first ekphrastic
representation: and there have been innumerable examples since
then: the final act of *The Winter's Tale*, Keats's "Ode on a Grecian
Urn," Baudelaire's "Le Masque," Yeats's "Sailing to Byzantium,"
Stevens's "Anecdote of the Jar," Williams's *Paterson* V, and
Lowell's "Marriage," to name only a few.[11] *Ekphrases*, although
they may refer to real or imaginary works of art, are first and
foremost texts: artistic works translated into words and put in the

service of a metaphorical, rhetorical, emblematic, allegorical, or moral intention. Auden's ekphrastic recreation, for example, of Achilles' shield, contrasting the pastoral and socially harmonious images of Homer's original to the images of a brutalized and war-ravaged countryside engraved in a contemporary shield, makes an explicitly moral statement about the nature of human conduct in the twentieth century. Other poets have used *ekphrasis* to describe allegorically the nature of art or poetry; one need only think of Keats addressing the eternal urn, or Baudelaire reacting with horror when an anamorphic statue of an elegant and sensuous woman reveals a hidden face in great anguish ("Le Masque").

The importing of a work of plastic art into a poem by means of rhetorical and poetic description imparts to the literary work a spatiality and immobility it normally does not have. *Ekphrasis* tends to still the temporal activity, the forward momentum, of the poem, Murray Krieger argues in his essay "*Ekphrasis* and the Still Movement of Poetry; or, *Laokoön* Revisited."[12] The imitation of a work of plastic art in literature enables the poet to find a metaphor, an emblematic correlative, by which to embody the dialectical relationship between spatiality and temporality that every poem implicitly presents and which Krieger calls "poetry's ekphrastic principle" (p. 6). *Ekphrasis* involves the use of "a plastic object as a symbol of the frozen, stilled world of plastic relationships which must be superimposed upon literature's turning world to 'still' it" (p. 5). The "ekphrastic dimension of literature," he writes, is evident "wherever the poem takes on the 'still' elements of plastic form which we normally attribute to the spatial arts" (p. 6). The ekphrastic object is a metaphor for the way the poem celebrates and arrests its movements. Krieger shows that poetry is simultaneously frozen and flowing, that it orders "spatial stasis within its temporal dynamics" (p. 24) by creating a spatial roundness and circularity through internal relations, echoes, and repetitions that unroll in time. *Ekphrasis* makes evident, therefore, "the spatiality and plasticity of literature's temporality" (p. 5).

Yet how striking the difference is between Ashbery's perpetually moving poetic world in "Self-Portrait" and the stilled temporal movement of poetry as Krieger describes it. The ekphrastic presence, in Ashbery's poem, of the Parmigianino painting, with its air of eternal completeness and static perfection, does not still the poem's temporal flow. In fact, the painting becomes the occasion for an escape from spatial immobility, a departure from the time-bounded stillness of poetry's ekphrastic principle. Parmigianino's overly centered convex painting cannot stop the centrifugal motion of the self-decentering poem, the multiple displacements of which occur in harmony with the temporal changes of the poet's errant consciousness that thinks, feels, and speaks in concert with the rhythms of Being. By bringing an ekphrastic object into the poem and then refusing to allow it to do what it normally would do—namely, according to Krieger, to immobilize and transfix the poem until it too becomes an object—Ashbery keeps his poetic expression free from the contamination of art's immobility, something that his prosy, conversational, run-on, nonrepetitive style of writing also succeeds in doing in regards to the potentially stilling effect of poetic diction, syntax, and prosody. It is the interiority enacted in "Self-Portrait in a Convex Mirror" that makes ekphrastic immobility impossible; the ekphrastic object is perpetually in movement, swerving in and out of the poet's consciousness; it never has time to lie still, to settle or harden into a solid object. Ashbery's decentered representation of the sixteenth-century painting and his mobile, discontinuous *ekphrasis* call into question the stillness and the temporal petrification of artistic representation and the very idea of temporal immobility itself, for as Ashbery writes in reference to the stilled scene in a photograph, "one cannot guard, treasure / That stalled moment; it too is flowing, fleeting" ("Syringa," *HD*, p. 70).

"Self-Portrait in a Convex Mirror" belongs to that group of ekphrastic poems that self-reflexively make a statement about the nature of poetry or art. Ashbery's poem initiates its mirroring of the Parmigianino painting in the following way:

> As Parmigianino did it, the right hand
> Bigger than the head, thrust at the viewer
> And swerving easily away, as though to protect
> What it advertises. A few leaded panes, old beams,

Fur, pleated muslin, a coral ring run together
In a movement supporting the face, which swims
Toward and away like the hand
Except that it is in repose. It is what is
Sequestered.

("SP," p. 68)

In these fragmentary perceptions, none of which make a
complete sentence except for the last, Ashbery quickly sums up
the painting's features. Quoting Vasari, he explains how
Parmigianino had a wooden convex surface made equal in size to
his convex mirror and "'set himself / With great art to copy all
that he saw in the glass'" (p. 68). Ashbery will repeatedly
question this idea of representing *all* that one sees, thus
uncovering the illusions of totality and detemporalized
wholeness which such representations contain. Paintings like the
Parmigianino self-portrait hide the fact that they have come into
existence through arbitrary selections made by the painter from
among his perceptions, thoughts, and feelings. Ashbery is aware
of the important events and impressions that had to be left out in
the process of creating the representation—this leaving-out
business," he calls it in an early poem ("The Skaters," *RM*, p.
39)—exclusions that point to the unreality and the solipsism of
totalized representations.[13]
    The reductiveness of the Parmigianino self-portrait is not the
only flaw Ashbery has discovered; there is also the painting's
lifelessness, its static unreality. Repeatedly, Ashbery refers to the
protected, embalmed, sequestered, imprisoned face of the
painter, surrounded at the painting's base by the large, curved
right hand, which is elongated and slightly distorted by the
convex surface. This hand both welcomes and defends, seeming
simultaneously to move out to greet the viewer and to retreat,
"Roving back to the body of which it seems / So unlikely a part,
to fence in and shore up the face" (p. 69). The painting
represents an autonomous and complete life within its convex
globe. But the price paid to bring forth this unified and coherent
image is high: it entails the deadening of the painter's spirit and
the sacrifice of his freedom. In representing himself,
Parmigianino has had to exclude much about his life and world

that must have defined him as a person. He has had to reduce his being to a miniature image which conforms to the limits of an artful and timeless prison. Parmigianino's is a cautious self-portrait, and in his striving for a perfect, idealized expression of himself, he distorts the meaning of human existence.

NOTES

11. For a study of the history of *ekphrasis*, see Jean H. Hagstrum, *The Sister Arts: The Tradition of Literary Pictorialism and English Poetry from Dryden to Gray* (Chicago, 1958), esp. pp. 17–29. Also, Svetlana Leontief Alpers, "*Ekphrasis* and Aesthetic Attitudes in Yasari's *Lives*," *Journal of the Warburg and Courtauld Institutes*, 23, Nos. 3–4 (1960), 190–215.

12. In *The Poet as Critic*, ed. Frederick P. W. McDowell (Evanston, 1967), pp. 3–26; rpt. in Murray Krieger, *The Play and Place of Criticism* (Baltimore, 1967), pp. 105–28.

13. Because of what it does not include, the poem, Ashbery suggests, is always an incomplete fragment of the moment or the life that has created it. It is a "part of something larger than itself which is the consciousness that produced it at that moment and which left out all kinds of things in the interests of writing the poem, which one is nevertheless aware of in the corners of the poem." "Craft Interview with John Ashbery," in *The Craft of Poetry: Interviews from The New York Quarterly*, ed. William Packard (Garden City, N.Y., 1974), p. 127.

    —Richard Stamelman, "Critical Reflections: Poetry and Art Criticism in Ashbery's "Self-Portrait in a Convex Mirror," *New Literary History* 15:3 (Spring 1984): 613–616.

LEE EDELMAN ON TITULAR QUANDARIES

[Lee Edelman is a Professor of English at Tufts University. He is the author of numerous articles on literary theory and twentieth-century poetry as well as several books, including *Transmemberment of Song: Hart Crane's Anatomies of Rhetoric and Desire*. In this excerpt, Edelman explorers the potential for the poem's title alone to throw into doubt the very nature of self-representation.]

"Self-Portrait in a Convex Mirror": the very title poses the problem raised by Ashbery's poem—a problem that itself might be formulated in terms of posing and imposture, a vocabulary of disguise that introduces doubt into the representation of the self. The title, of course, announces the text's engagement of the issue of representation and, specifically, of the difficulties that inhere in the attempt to represent oneself. For the image constitutive of a self-portrait demands that it be read in some relation to the original; but as Ashbery's poem indicates, the nature of the "original" is often far from clear. Douglas Crase has suggested that Ashbery's "Self-Portrait" points to the convexity or distortion implicit in any enterprise of self-depiction.[1] By carrying Crase's observation one step further, however, we may note that the effect of convexity in Ashbery's "Self-Portrait" is to redirect attention from the portrait of the "self" to the distinctive *angle* of that portrayal. The subject, then, is less the portraitist than the problematic nature of the portraiture; for the text announces the self-portrait's generic imperative to mirror not the "self," but the process of mirroring the "self," its persistent concern, in other words, with the representation of (self) representation.

Since the attempt to represent representation, however, always finds itself mediated by anterior representations, the self-portrait can only offer its representation of representation as an interpretation of an earlier representation of representation. We have entered, then, a hall of mirrors, or in Joyce's words from *Ulysses*, "a mirror within a mirror." And as a result, the vexing convexity of Ashbery's aesthetic "mirror" may seem, if not to have invested itself and thereby become concave, to have conned us at any rate into Plato's cave where the shadows of shadows beguile us with a seemingly endless chain of displacements.

Critics who would place themselves in control of this process try to twist that chain upon itself by defining its circuit as "self-reflexive."[2] But the inadequacy of that term to the situation at hand becomes obvious if one attends carefully to the system of displacements here at work. For if the representation of the "self" is, in fact, a representation of the representation of the "self," and *that* representation is, in turn, an interpretation of some other representation of some other "self," the identity of the "*self*" is too gravely in doubt to allow this process to be explained away as neatly "self-reflexive." Instead, we must ask with the seriousness latent in all rhetorical questions (to the extent that they constitute questions of rhetoric): who is it that Ashbery's "Self-Portrait" actually portrays?

Asking such a question inevitably leads back to the title and to the question raised by the title—a question that takes shape as a question *of* title. For we trust ask ourselves who has title to this title, and what entitles Ashbery to appropriate it as his own. The title that names the poem, that seems to identify its distinctive property, bestows upon the text the proper name of another, thus providing the property with a name that is, as it turns out, not strictly proper. It is Parmigianino, of course, who is entitled to this title beneath which Ashbery's poem poses as if it were its own. And Ashbery, from the outset, acknowledges the painter's prior claim, beginning his own "Self-Portrait": "As Parmigianino did it."[3] By presenting his poem under the name of Parmigianino's painting, Ashbery seems to indicate that the earlier work of art serves, in some sense, as the model for his own artistic endeavor.

But this too leads to complications. What, after all; does it mean for something to serve as a "model"? In the domain of the plastic arts—the domain suggested by Parmigianino's "Self-Portrait"—a model may be that person or object that the work of art attempts to imitate, the original that the creation seeks to double or reproduce. Yet if the model possesses the priority and the authenticity that derive from its status as the "original," the word "model," in another sense, implies a crucial *lack* of authenticity to the extent that it signifies a reproduction of some *other* object, a replica or a copy, frequently on a scale much smaller than that of what it represents. The "Self-Portrait in a Convex Mirror"—both a title and as genre—becomes, in this way. a machine for the production of reproductions claiming title as "originals": and the title of Ashbery's poem, therefore, by designating Parmigianino's self-portrait as its model, only inscribes an uncertainty into all of the relationships opening out from that title—an undecidability that centers on question of authenticity and imposture.

Once more, then, we return to the title, this time to view it in relation to the text; but to do so we must consider first the poetics of the title, an issue central to Ashbery's investigations of the issue of centrality. Ashbery himself, in interviews, has discussed the importance of titles and the role that they play in the creation of his poetry.[4] In *As We Know* he calls attention to this concern in a group of poems, each of which takes shape as a single sentence played cut across the title and the single line of the poem's text proper. One, for example, is called "The Cathedral Is" and it consists of one line: "Slated for demolition." Such a work forces us to interrogate the nature of any title. It forces us to suspend our assumption that a title like "Self-Portrait in a Convex Mirror" will be metaphoric—a large box to contain the poem by means of some essential correspondence—and to consider the possibility that it may announce a purely metonymic relationship—a relationship governed only by chance or contiguity. It compels us, therefore, to question the *place* of the title. Is it situated outside the text, presiding over it from a privileged, authoritative position to enunciate the text's authentic name—the name that articulates its essential character? Or is the title itself inside the text, and thus far from being conclusive, or privileged, or authentic, always necessarily partial, always necessarily *textual*? To put the matter another way, we must ask not only if the title names the text properly, but also if the title is, properly, a name at all.

To ask in what way "Self-Portrait in a Convex Mirror" names Ashbery's poem, then, is to begin to bring into relation the various differences that inhabit the title—differences between Parmigianino and Ashbery, between representation and misrepresentation, between metaphor and metonymy. It is to recognize that the title, insofar as it identifies the literary object by bestowing a name upon it, aspires to the patriarchal prerogative of the proper name. A sexual thematics thus informs the questioning of the title that has been raised in terms of rhetoric above. That is to say, if the title can be placed in a metaphoric relation to the text, if it can assume, to use Roman Jakobson's term, a "paradigmatic" function so that Ashbery's poem can be seen to *be*, or to be *like*, a self-portrait in a convex mirror, then the title can be said to name the text "properly," to identify it legitimately in terms of resemblance or correspondence. This association of metaphor with the production—or the reproduction—of legitimate substitutes springs, as Jonathan Culler points out, from the privileged position that patriarchal cultures accord "metaphorical relations—relations of resemblance between separate items that can be substituted for one another, such as obtain between the father and the miniature replica with the same name, the child."[5]

As a metaphor, then, the title would claim an essentially phallic authority as superscription. It would participate in a system of patriarchal values centering on the determinacy of truth, on the certainty of origins, and, indeed, on the very notion of centrality itself. It is that system, with is emphasis on truth as presence and as unity, a system underwritten by the visibility and "presence" of the phallus, that Derrida has labeled "phallogocentrism."[6] By seeing the phallus as implicated in the nostalgia for presence at work in logocentrism, Derrida, as he himself makes explicit, takes aim at Lacan and at what he sees as Lacan's concept of the phallus as a transcendental or "privileged signifier," as that which grounds or gives meaning to the play of all other signifiers.[7] In opposition to such a designation of the phallus as primary and unique, Derrida declares, "It is one and the same system: the erection of a paternal logos ... and the phallus as 'privileged signifier' (Lacan)."[8] Thus insofar as the title as a metaphor seeks to define the text in terms of essence or essential correspondence, it aspires to the phallic authority central to phallogocentrism. And in so doing it asserts the legitimacy and the intelligibility of text that it seeks to name by affirming the certainty of its paternity, the unmistakable resemblance it bears to its origin.

Yet as the questions raised earlier have already made clear, the legitimacy of this title as a name for the text is precisely what remains uncertain. For the title here, to the extent that it functions metonymically rather than metaphorically, rejects the vertical hierarchy of Jakobson's paradigmatic relations in favor of the more random, horizontal displacements of a syntagmatic chain. We can see this by noting that the title of Ashbery's poem does not merely stand over the text magisterially, designating the poem as "Self-Portrait in a Convex Mirror." It simultaneously finds itself implicated in the syntactical structure of the opening line, thus disseminating itself and denying any claim to the superior authority of a privileged, determinate meaning. After all, the text's initial clause, "As Parmigianino did it" (*SP*, p. 68), refers to the poem's effort to self-representation only by directing us back to the title for the antecedent of "it." Through its involvement in the syntax of these opening words, the title can be viewed as having an aleatory rather than an essential relation to the text. And if, in its metonymic relation to the poem, the title refuses to concentrate meaning, but disseminates it instead, it is appropriate that it does so by raising the question of antecedents or origins. For dissemination, as Derrida has discussed it, calls origin into question insofar as it is that which does not return to the father—which does not accede to the singularity and intelligibility of "Truth."

NOTES

1. Douglas Crase, "The Prophetic Ashbery," *Beyond Amazement: New Essays on John Ashbery*, ed. David Lehman (Ithaca: Cornell Univ. Press, 1980), p. 42.

2. Ashbery himself has said of his work: "As has been pointed out by Richard Howard, among others, my poems are frequently commenting on themselves as they're getting written." ("Craft Interview with John Ashbery," *The Craft of Poetry: Interviews from the New York Quarterly*, ed. William Packard [Garden City, N.Y.: Doubleday, 1974], p. 121). This essay will suggest that such an assertion ought not to be accepted unquestioningly. Instead it should be investigated as thoroughly as an author's more conventional thematic readings of his own work.

3. John Ashbery, "Self-Portrait in a Convex Mirror," *Self-Portrait in a Convex Mirror* (New York: Penguin Books, 1976), p. 68. The poem will hereafter be abbreviated as *SP* and all further page references will be given parenthetically in the text.

4. Ashbery writes: "It seems to me that the title is something that tips the whole poem in one direction or another ..." ("Craft Interview," p. 111).

5. Jonathan Culler, *On Deconstruction: Theory and Criticism after Structuralism* (Ithaca: Cornell Univ. Press, 1982), p. 60.

6. See Jacques Derrida, *Éperons, Les Styles de Nietzsche*, trans. Barbara Harlow (Chicago: Univ. of Chicago Press, 1979), p. 60. The French "phallogocentrisme" is mistranslated as phallocentrism on the facing page.

7. Jacques Lacan, *Érits: A Selection*, trans. Alan Sheridan (New York: Norton, 1977), p. 287.

8. Cited in Culler, *On Deconstruction*, p. 172.

—Lee Edelman, "The Pose of Imposture: Ashbery's 'Self Portrait in a Convex Mirror,'" *Twentieth Century Literature* 32:1 (Spring 1986): 95–99.

[Thomas Gardner is a Professor of English at Virginia Polytechnic Institute and State University. In addition to *Regions of Unlikeness: Explaining Contemporary Poetry* and the study of Whitman's poetic descendants, from which the following is extracted, he is the author of numerous articles on modern poetry. Here he explicates the poem's central dilemma.]

"Self-Portrait" is, first, a deliberate attempt to learn how to live in something other. In the "winding" speculations initiated by his encounter with a puzzling mirror painting, Ashbery deliberately enters and weaves together the rich polyphony of ways of speaking that radiate from, and create something of, that moment. What is most significant is that this rich weave of voices, this elaborate detailing of the self, is brought about by what I have called Ashbery's self-monitoring or his doubleness. As he continually calls attention to the medium's distance from himself, he also gives himself a way in which to use it more forcefully. Just as Whitman had to acknowledge his distance from the stallion before "using" it—or Roethke's his from the sea, or Duncan's his from the ensemble—so Ashbery's doubleness enables him to step back from, and then more richly work, the medium through which he speaks.[9] And one can go even further, for although the medium being embraced through much of this poem is a single painting, we realize by the end of the work that what is true about the hold of Parmigianino's self-portrait on Ashbery is finally even more applicable to the more extensive medium of language itself.

As the poem begins, Ashbery, "The dreaming model / In the silence of the studio," is considering "Lifting the pencil to the self-portrait" (SP, 71). Parmigianino's painting seems to seize and focus those dreams by, at first, offering a positive example of how one might go about shaping and articulating that humming commentary.[10] What the painter did was very simple:

> Vasari says, "Francesco one day set himself
> To take his own portrait, looking at himself for that purpose
> In a convex mirror, such as is used by barbers ...

He accordingly caused a ball of wood to be made
By a turner, and having divided it in half and
Brought it to the size of the mirror, he set himself
With great art to copy all that he saw in the glass,"
Chiefly his reflection, of which the portrait
Is the reflection once removed.

(SP, 68)

Vasari's description emphasizes the artistic mastery of Parmigianino's attempt to look at himself: he "caused" the ball to be made, "divided it," "brought it to ... size," and copied what was clearly labeled a reflection "with great art," the series of verbs suggesting a confidence in technique. When Ashbery muses in the poem's opening line that he might *embrace* a version of the painter's painstaking art and, "As Parmigianino did it" (SP, 68), develop a method to look at and copy his own reflections, he means to borrow that confident mastery.[11] The rounded surface of the mirror and the painter's pose before it ("we have surprised him / At work" [SP, 74]) create a distortion in which the face seems to peer out from deep within the wooden globe. This deliberately chosen method of representation seems, on a first reading, to be a signal of technique's ability to master flux. Both the hand in the foreground grasping the ball and the locked-together details of the studio's background ("a coral ring"—a reef) appear as signs of protection. In separating one aspect of the self from its constantly moving world, then, art preserves what would ordinarily dissolve by giving it boundaries:

the right hand

Bigger than the head, thrust at the viewer
And swerving easily away, as though to protect
What it advertises. A few leaded panes, old beams,
Fur, pleated muslin, a coral ring run together
In a movement supporting the face, which swims
Toward and away like the hand
Except that it is in repose. It is what is
Sequestered.

(SP, 68)

Because what it advertizes—what it attractively represents to us—is protected and separated, then, the face in the painting will always retain its qualities at that moment; it will remain luminous, alive, and whole: "The time of day or the density of the light / Adhering to the face keeps it / Lively and intact in a recurring wave / Of arrival. The soul establishes itself" (SP, 68).

However, as David Kalstone points out, this initial embrace is rapidly revised, the face's distance from the surface (a boundary seemingly marked by the hand) suggesting a second, and more disturbing, reading:[12]

> The surface
> Of the mirror being convex, the distance increases
> Significantly; that is, enough to make the point
> That the soul is a captive, treated humanely, kept
> In suspension, unable to advance much farther
> Than your look as it intercepts the picture.
>
> (SP, 68–69)

That this surface holds the face at a greater remove than a flat piece of glass suggests that, in protecting the soul, the painter has had to make it a captive, permanently sequestering it from the moving world of which it was a part. In order to study the face, Parmigianino has had to restrain it forcibly: "The soul has to stay where it is, / Even though restless, hearing raindrops at the pane, / The sighing of autumn leaves thrashed by the wind, / Longing to be free, outside, but it must stay / Posing in this place" (SP, 69). And if this is true, the "soul" represented is no soul at all; unchanging, motionless, cut off from the secret world that has nourished its pose, the painting is a diminished thing: "The secret is too plain. The pity of it smarts, / Makes hot tears spurt: that the soul is not a soul, / Has no secret, is small, and it fits / Its hollow perfectly: its room, our moment of attention" (SP, 69). The hot tears are Ashbery's, for, having realized that in this painting "we see only postures of the dream" (SP, 69) and not those dimensionless stirrings of the dream itself, he now reads the foregrounded hand as a warning addressed to him:

> it is life englobed.
> One would like to stick one's hand
> Out of the globe, but its dimension,

What carries it, will not allow it.
No doubt it is this, not the reflex
To hide something, which makes the hand loom large
As it retreats slightly.

(SP, 69)

The painter's hand seems to be pressing futilely against the surface of the globe, distorting under its attempt to get out. If so, the painting becomes a warning to other artists that the medium—"its dimension, / What carries it"—used to englobe a life so that it can be seen has also frozen and distorted it. To the poet, the painting no longer offers the promise that it is possible to isolate and protect experience, but rather that statement that there is no true reflection: "There is no way / To build it flat" (SP, 69).[13] As with the openings of all the poems we have been concerned with in this study, then, the promise of embracing one's experience directly is simply put aside.

Given the implications of this newly understood argument for his own task—if he creates "As Parmigianino did," he will have trapped himself within the distortion of his own reflective medium—it is not surprising that Ashbery's immediate response is a personal appeal to the painter to break loose from that threatening position: "Francesco, your hand is big enough / To wreck the sphere, and too big, / One would think, to weave delicate meshes / That only argue its further detention" (SP, 70). But then, shockingly, he realizes that there is no Francesco to address—there is only a painted surface, neither encouraging him to use its method as a model nor warning him of its dangers.[14] Separation from the viewer's concerns—otherness—seems, finally, to be what the distortion has been signalling:

your eyes proclaim

That everything is surface. The surface is what's there
And nothing can exist except what's there.
There are no recesses in the room, only alcoves,
And the window doesn't matter much, or that
Sliver of window or mirror on the right, even
As a gauge of the weather, which in French is
Le temps, the word for time

(SP, 70)

By blurring the recesses behind the painter and declaring the movements of time and weather to be nonsignificant, the painting has eliminated reference to any world beyond its aesthetic surface. Because there is no depth, the notion of a "soul" inviting the poet in or straining to break free seems curiously irrelevant. If this is the case, Ashbery's previous "words for the surface," based as they were on the assumption that art makes a "core" of the self visible and can thus be interpreted in personal terms, become simply his own speculations. Like the mirror painting, his own unraveled words are equally distortions, abortive snatches at an illusive meaning: "The words are only speculation / (From the Latin *speculum*, mirror): / They seek and cannot find the meaning of the music." He is left with no guidance about how to shape his buzzing, drifting experience: "And just as there are no words for the surface, that is, / No words to say what it really is, that it is not / Superficial but a visible core, then there is / No way out of the problem of pathos vs. experience" (SP, 70). What he has learned is that the painting is "neither embrace nor warning," but a third thing that is separate from him—a neutral surface "which holds something of both in pure / Affirmation that doesn't affirm anything" (SP, 70).

NOTES

9. Although Parmigianino's work is, in a sense, an already internalized voice and Ashbery's patient unfolding of it simply an expanded version of what normally goes on in the internal "bounding from air to air" of all his poems, Ashbery's uncharacteristic focus on a single object's way of speaking helps the reader visualize the imaginative activity implied by his other work. Ashbery supports the idea that the painting can be considered an already internalized voice: "I had always meant to do something about that painting because it haunted me for so long." See *American Poetry Observed*, ed. Joe David Bellamy (Urbana: University of Illinois Press, 1986), p. 17. Altieri, *Self and Sensibility*, p. 115, also comments on the uniqueness of this poem's slow unfolding.

10. David Kalstone, in *Five Temperaments* (New York: Oxford University Press, 1977), writes: "The speaker in 'Self-Portrait' appears to 'happen' upon Parmigianino's painting as a solution to a problem pondered before the poem begins" (p. 176). Kalstone's reading of the poem's opening section is particularly strong.

11. Several critics have noted the connection between Parmigianino's reflection in the mirror and Ashbery's on the page. See, for example, Kalstone, *Five Temperaments*, p. 177.

12. Ibid., pp. 176–77. Accounting for the speaker's changing readings of the painting is a key interpretive decision in working with the poem, as studying the three strongest discussions of the poem will demonstrate. Kalstone and Richard Stamelman, "Critical Reflections: Poetry and Art Criticism in Ashbery's 'Self-Portrait in a Convex Mirror,'" *New Literary History* 15 (Spring 1984): 607–30, treat the painting as a celebration of the "powers of foreshortening and concentration" (Kalstone, p. 180) or an expression of "faith in the representability of world and self through art" (Stamelman, p. 611). The speaker's different readings, then, illustrate his struggles in accepting or, ultimately, rejecting this fixed view. Altieri sees in the painting "multiple contexts"—a variety of "expressive energies" that help prompt the "various ways the speaker sees himself in the painting," all of which are significant in Ashbery's explorations of the counterbalancing energies of "the processes of thinking" (p. 151). As my own reading will make clear, I also see the speaker's different readings as prompted, in at least some sense, by the painting's own metaphors.

13. I take this to be a statement Parmigianino was fully conscious of making in his initial choice of such an obviously distorted reflecting medium. That Parmigianino thus calls attention to the "difference" involved in his act of self-representation makes it difficult to read this poem, as Stamelman does for example, as simply the author's "radical criticism of the illusions and deceptions inherent in forms of traditional representation"—with Parmigianino defending the accuracy of reflection. Nevertheless, I agree with him on the position the poem finally arrives at: that "painting and poetry can represent nothing other than their own difficult, often thwarted efforts at representation" (p. 611).

14. I was aided in seeing this by Helen Vendler's analysis of "Ode on a Grecian Urn," a poem that clearly stands behind Ashbery's. See *The Odes of John Keats* (Cambridge: Harvard University Press, 1983), pp. 116–52.

—Thomas Gardner, *Discovering Ourselves in Whitman: The Contemporary American Long Poem* (Urbana: University of Illinois Press, 1989): 148–152.

"Wet Casements"

As we have seen in "Self-Portrait," a reflection, especially a distorted one, is a potent metaphor for Ashbery. In "Wet Casements" he takes that trope one step further, situating the reflection in the subjective eyes of others and, in doing so, creates another kind of double mirror in which a reader's interpretation reveals as much about the reader as it does the originating poem or poet. Harold Bloom sees in the concluding two lines a heroic and canonical reassertion of the distinctly American right to solitude and self-definition. Others, such as Geoff Ward, hear more than a hint of irony in the poem and argue the exact opposite—that Ashbery is in fact writing about the impossibility of a "single, discrete self." As always, Ashbery himself remains suspended in the continuum, more interested in the debate than the outcome.

At least that's how it seems at the poem's outset, where the speaker displays a calculated neutrality: "The concept is interesting." But it remains merely conceptual only until things get personal in the fifth line and the "you in falbalas / Of some distant but not too distant era" (a "falbala" is a festooned flounce on a woman's gown, or more generically, any bit of showy trimming; here Ashbery is probably using the word, together with "cosmetics," as a coy reference to homosexual flamboyance) are startled out of your studied pose by the sound of your name dropped "at some crowded cocktail / Party" and you are forced to wonder just what is being said about you, whether that representation of you might take on a life of its own, and just how much self-image is defined by external referents.

Like the "ghostly transparent face" superimposed atop "the look of others through / Their own eyes," Ashbery implicitly overlays this generalized social quandary, to which anyone can relate, with a series of telescoping contexts that simultaneously give the poem both a greater intimacy and a broader resonance. The next largest of these contexts is artistic influence. One of the primary strategies critics use to apprehend a unique new artist is to find aesthetic analogs and extrapolate common aims and traits. The result is a gradual diffusion of the artist's individuality and a loss of control over definition of self. From the beginning of his career, Ashbery has suffered this fate. Auden, in his introduction to *Some Trees*, likens Ashbery to Rimbaud and other French Surrealists. Bloom, and many others, trace Ashbery's lineage back through Stevens to Whitman and the Transcendentalists. David Lehman places him firmly in the New York School, while others situate his artistic origins "across the pond" with Auden, Eliot, and Pound. Ashbery himself claims he is as likely to draw inspiration from a tabloid or overheard conversation as from an established body of work. He also said something very telling once in an interview, which, though tongue-in-cheek, speaks directly to the effacing effect of the critic's need to categorize and the artist's conflicting desire for self-definition: "I'm sometimes kind of jealous of my work. It keeps getting all the attention and I'm not. After all, I wrote it."

An even more personalized subdivision of this context of influence concerns Ashbery's professional situation at the time he wrote the poem. Despite winning major literary prizes and generating a lot of laudatory press, Ashbery's cachet remained (and remains to this day) controversial. As Peter Stitt puts it in his *Uncertainty and Plenitude*, "What makes this muchness of recognition odd is the fact that so many serious readers of poetry seem to have no idea of what Ashbery's poems are about." Couple the fear of being misunderstood and defined merely by influence with the minority status of a homosexual and further compound the issue with the philosophical uncertainty that one's self can ever be conclusively defined without destroying that which is most fundamentally human and you have some pretty heady subject matter for a poet purported to have none.

Identifying the poem's subject matter, however, proves much easier than pinning down Ashbery's stance *towards* that subject matter. Three viewpoints are portrayed and explored—denial, desire, and detachment—yet all are undercut by a tone of ironic self-doubt. The poem's speaker begins in denial, thinking he can treat the opinions of others as a mere "concept," thereby avoiding any emotional fallout. This stance is quickly replaced by a more honest desire (and anger when that desire is thwarted) to know exactly what "epistemological snapshot" of him people are carrying around: "I want that information very much today, // Can't have it, and this makes me angry." Once again, as in "Soonest Mended," Ashbery uses the word "information" as a trope for what is un-communicated and out of reach, emphasizing the point typographically with a stanza break. This desire for "information" and anger at not getting it catalyzes the determination "to build a bridge like that / Of Avignon, on which people may dance for the feeling / Of dancing on a bridge." In referring to a French children's song ("Sur Le Pont D'Avignon") about men and women dancing on the famous bridge, Ashbery is perhaps alluding to a simpler stage of life, before self-consciousness set in. By willfully re-inhabiting that mindset, the speaker hopes to become whole again: "I shall at last see my *complete* face / Reflected not in the water but in the worn stone floor of *my* bridge" (my emphasis). This sense of wholeness, in turn, gives way to confident closure and detachment: "I shall keep to myself. / I shall not repeat others' comments about me." There the poem ends, but as John Shoptaw and others point out, clues in grammar, tone, and Ashbery's choice of metaphor suggest an ironic undermining of this final assertion. The deliberate repetition of "shall" reminds readers that all these things have yet to happen. It also reminds us of those better-known commandments, none of which have been followed to the letter. Subtler is the typographic separation, in the last two lines, of "I" from "myself" and "me," suggesting a lingering disassociation of identity. Even more sublimated is the undercurrent of irony that flows beneath these lines like a Cartesian spring. No evidence of it exists above ground (save perhaps the affinity of those two sentences with the facile affirmations of self-help books, a source Ashbery would almost certainly satirize), and yet, the high concentration of irony elsewhere in Ashbery's oeuvre forces it to the surface. Lastly, we have Ashbery's choice of metaphor—dancing on a bridge "like that / Of Avignon." On first reading this sounds like a heroically romantic gesture, this creation of place where people can be free of their self-image anxieties and see their "complete face(s)," but the Avignon bridge was partially felled by a 17th-century flood and now can only take you part of the way across. Surely the obsessively observant author of "Self-Portrait" would not fail to take this fact into account.

Thus, after moving through denial, desire, and detachment, the poem ends up in a kind of purgatorial afterlife, in which the mystery of identity remains unsolved and the Self becomes the "Ghostly transparent face" alluded to earlier, unfixed and overlaying a "digest" of "impressions" that will require continued revisions and indexing. In Ashbery's universe, it seems, the only cosmological constant is the certainty of uncertainty. An interesting concept indeed.

"Wet Casements"

HAROLD BLOOM ON THE TROPE OF AMERICAN SOLITUDE

[In this extract from an essay that originally appeared in *Agon: Towards a Theory of Revisionism* (1982), Bloom situates the poem within an American poetic tradition celebrating solitude and the freedom of self-definition.]

I heard Ashbery's poem *Wet Casements* read aloud by its poet at Yale, before I had seen the text. Only the pathos of the traditional phrase "immortal wound" seems to me adequate to my response, both immediate and continuing. For me, it had joined the canon, directly I had heard it, and it transcended the poet's customary, beautifully evasive, rather flat delivery. What persuaded me, cognitively and emotionally, was the poem's immediate authority in taking up and transuming the major American trope of "solitude," in the peculiar sense that Emerson invented, by way of misprision out of Montaigne. Montaigne, in his essay *Of Solitude*, warned that "this occupation with books is as laborious as any other, and as much an enemy to health." But American solitude seems to be associated always with bookish ideals, even if not directly with books, from Emerson and Thoreau to the present moment. Emerson, in his essay *The Transcendentalist*, prophesied that his disciples would choose solitude:

> They are lonely; the spirit of their writing and conversation is lonely; they repel influences; they shun general society; they incline to shut themselves in their chamber in the house....

It seems a more accurate prophecy of Emily Dickinson than of Walt Whitman, but that is because Whitman's *persona*, his mask, was so profoundly deceptive. Though Whitman proclaims companionship, his poetry opens to glory only in solitude, whether that be in the phantasmagoria of *The Sleepers*, in the struggles with his waxing and waning poetic self in the *Sea Drift* pieces, or more intensely in the uniquely solitary elegy for Lincoln, *When Lilacs Last in the Dooryard Bloom'd.*

The poetry of our century has its major spokesmen for solitude in Wallace Stevens and Robert Frost, both of whom flourished best when most perfectly alone. Stevens particularly is closest to a sense of triumph when he proclaims his isolation:

> In solitude the trumpets of solitude
> Are not of another solitude resounding;
> A little string speaks for a crowd of voices.

The darker side of solitude, the estrangement from life brought about by so literary an ideal, is more a burden of contemporary American poetry. Prophecy here belongs to Hart Crane, who drowned himself in 1932, three months before what would have been his thirty-third birthday. His elegy for himself, the immensely poignant *The Broken Tower*, possibly takes from Walter Pater's unfinished prose romance, *Gaston de Latour*, a beautiful phrase, "the visionary company," and converts it into an image of loss, of hopeless quest:

> And so it was I entered the broken world
> To trace the visionary company of love....

Such a tracing would have taken the poet beyond solitude, but Crane's life and work ended more in the spirit of his late poem *Purgatorio*, which pictures the poet in exile and apart, cut off from country and from friends.

The contemporary poet John Ashbery is the culmination of this very American solitude. His recent poem *Wet Casements* records the loss of a beloved name, or perhaps just the name of someone once loved, and then expresses the creative anger of a consciousness condemned to a solitude of lost information, or a world of books. "Anger" becomes Ashbery's substitute word or trope for what Montaigne and Emerson called "solitude":

> I shall use my anger to build a bridge like that
> Of Avignon, on which people may dance for the feeling

Of dancing on a bridge. I shall at last see my complete face
Reflected not in the water but in the worn stone floor of my
bridge.

Is this not the most American of solitudes, where even the
self's own reflection is to be observed, not in nature, but in the
self's own solitary creation? The solitude that Montaigne both
praised and warned against, but which Emerson wholly exalted,
attains a climax in Ashbery's final lines:

I shall keep to myself.
I shall not repeat others' comments about me.

Indeed, no American feels free when she or he is not alone, and
it may be the eloquent sorrow of America that it must continue,
in its best poems, to equate freedom with solitude. (...)

Ashbery shies away from epigraphs, yet *Wet Casements* turns to
Kafka's *Wedding Preparations in the Country* in order to get started.
The epigraph though is more about not getting started:

When Eduard Raban, coming along the passage, walked into the
open doorway, he saw that it was raining. It was not raining much.

Three paragraphs on from this opening, Raban stares at a lady
who perhaps has looked at him:

She did so indifferently, and she was perhaps, in any case, only
looking at the falling rain in front of him or at the small
nameplates of firms that were fixed to the door over his head.
Raban thought she looked amazed. "Well," he thought, "if I could
tell her the whole story, she would cease to be astonished. One
works so feverishly at the office that afterwards one is too tired
even to enjoy one's holidays properly. But even all that work does
not give one a claim to be treated lovingly by everyone; on the
contrary, one is alone, a total stranger and only an object of
curiosity. And so long as you say 'one' instead of 'I' there's nothing
in it and one can easily tell the story; but as soon as you admit to
yourself that it is you yourself, you feel as though transfixed and
are horrified."

That dark reflection is the *ethos*, the universe of limitation, of the poem *Wet Casements*, whose opening irony swerves from Kafka's yet only to more self-alienation:

The conception is interesting: to see, as though reflected
In streaming windowpanes, the look of others through
Their own eyes.

"Interesting" is one of Ashbery's driest ironies, and is a trope for something like "desperate," while the "look of others through / Their own eyes" is an evasion, wholly characteristic of Ashbery's self-expression through his own reflexive seeing. Yet the conception is interesting, particularly since it is both concept and engendering. How much can one catch of the look of others or of the self, through their eyes or one's own, when the look is reflected in wet casements, in streaming windowpanes? The question is desperate enough, and the slightly archaic "casements" of the title means not just any windows opening outwards, but the casements of Keats's odes, open to the vision of romance. Keats concluded his *Ode to Psyche* with the vision of "A bright torch, and a casement ope at night, / To let the warm love in!" In *Ode to a Nightingale*, there is the still grander trope of the bird's song: "that oft-times hath / Charmed magic casements, opening on the foam / Of perilous seas in fairy lands forlorn." *Wet Casements* is a strange, late, meditative version of the Keatsian ode, obviously not in mere form, but in rhetorical stance. Perhaps we might describe it as Keats assimilated to the Age of Kafka, and still it remains Keats. Lest I seem more extreme even than usual, I turn to the merely useful point that must be made in starting to read Ashbery's poem. It could not be entitled *Wet Windows*, because these have to be windows that open outwards, just as Kafka's Raban walked into the open doorway to see that it was raining. There must be still, even in Kafka and in Ashbery, what there always was in Keats, the hope, however forlorn, of open vision, and of a passage to other selves.

Yet *Wet Casements* is a beautifully forlorn poem, a hymn to lost Eros, not an *Ode to Psyche* triumphantly opening to Eros even as a poem attempts closure. The conception is indeed interesting, to see the self-seen look of others reflected in a window closed against the rain, but that could and should be opened outwards in a season of calm weather. "A digest," Ashbery writes, meaning a daemonic division or distribution of self-images, ending with the overlay of his own "ghostly transparent face." We are back in one of Ashbery's familiar modes, from at least *Three Poems* on, a division of self and soul of a Whitmanian rather than Yeatsian kind, where "you" is Ashbery's soul or re-imagined character, in the process of becoming, and "I" is Ashbery's writing self or reduced personality. But the "you" is also the erotic possibility of otherness, now lost, or of a muse-figure never quite found. This is the "you" described in the long passage that is a single sentence and that takes up exactly half of the poem's length:

> You in falbalas
> Of some distant but not too distant era, the cosmetics,
> The shoes perfectly pointed, drifting (how long you
> Have been drifting; how long I have too for that matter)
> Like a bottle-imp toward a surface which can never be approached,
> Never pierced through into the timeless energy of a present
> Which would have its own opinions on these matters,
> Are an epistemological snapshot of the processes
> That first mentioned your name at some crowded cocktail
> Party long ago, and someone (not the person addressed)
> Overheard it and carried that name around in his wallet
> For years as the wallet crumbled and bills slid in
> And out of it.

Call it a Whitmanian "drifting," an episode in Ashbery's continuous, endless Song of Himself. "Drifting" is the crucial word in the passage, akin to Whitman's "sea-drift" elegiac intensities. What precisely can "drifting" mean here? "You"—soul of Ashbery, lost erotic partner, the other or muse component in lyric poetry— are attired in the ruffles, frills, cosmetics, ornamental shoes of a studied nostalgia, one of those eras Stevens said the imagination was always at an end of, a vanished elegance. Like an Arabian Nights bottle-imp you are drifting perpetually towards a fictively paradoxical surface, always absent. If it were present, if you could approach it ever, then you would be pierced through, you would have pierced through, into a true present, indeed into the ontological timelessness of an energy of consciousness that would pass judgment upon all drifting, have its own opinion, presumably negative, of drifting. Again, why "drifting"? The best clue is that the drifter is "an epistemological snapshot of the processes" of time itself, which has a wallet at its back, a crumbling wallet, with bills and alms for oblivion sliding in and out of it. The unreachable surface of a present would have timeless energy, but "drifting" means to yield with a wise passivity to temporal entropy, and so to be reduced to "an epistemological snapshot" of time's revenges.

Yet that is only part of a dialectic; the other part is naming, having been named, remembering, having been remembered. Your overheard name, carried round for years in time's wallet, may be only another alm for oblivion, and yet its survival inspires in you the poet's creative rage for immortality, or what Vico called "divination": "I want that information very much today, / Can't have it, and this makes me angry." The striking word is "information," reminding Ashbery's readers of the crucial use of that word in *Wet Casements*'s meditative rival, *Soonest Mended* in *The Double Dream of Spring*:

Only by that time we were in another chapter and confused
About how to receive this latest piece of information.
Was it information? Weren't we rather acting this out
For someone else's benefit, thoughts in a mind
With room enough and to spare for our little problems....

"Information" in both poems means a more reliable knowledge communicated by and from otherness, than is allowed by one's status as an epistemological snapshot of a drifter through temporal processes. But the casements do not open out to otherness and to love, and where information is lacking, only the proper use of the rage to order words remains:

I shall use my anger to build a bridge like that
Of Avignon, on which people may dance for the feeling
Of dancing on a bridge.

The round-song of the bridge of Avignon charmingly goes on repeating that the bridge is there, and that people dance upon it.

As a trope for the poem *Wet Casements*, this tells us both the limitation and the restituting strength of Ashbery's ambitions. But the song of the self, as in Whitman, movingly and suddenly ascends to a triumph:

> I shall at last see my complete face
> Reflected not in the water but in the worn stone floor of my
>   bridge.

The dancers are Ashbery's readers, who as Stevens once said of his elite, will do for the poet what he cannot do for himself: receive his poetry. Elegantly, Ashbery reverses his initial trope, where the reflection in streaming windowpanes did not allow seeing the complete face either of others or of the self. The worn stone floor of the bridge of words has replaced the wet casements, a substitution that prompts the strongest of all Ashberian poetic closures:

> I shall keep to myself.
> I shall not repeat others' comments about me.

If the sentiment is unlike Whitman's, its sermon-like directness still would have commended it to Whitman, or to Thoreau, or even to the Founder, Emerson. For this is the Emersonian Sublime, a belated declaration of self-reliance, or a repression of every fathering force, even the American ones.

—Harold Bloom, "Measuring the Canon: John Ashbery's 'Wet Casements' and 'Tapestry,'" *Agon* (Oxford: Oxford University Press, 1982).

DAVID BROMWICH ON THE DISTANCE FROM "ONE" TO "I"

[David Bromwich is a Professor of English at Yale University. Among other works, he is the author of *Skeptical Music: Essays on Modern Poetry* and *Disowned by Memory: Wordsworth's Poetry of the 1790's*. In this extract, Bromwich expands on the poem's epigraph and uses Kafka's unpublished story as an entry point into the poem.]

If these comments on image and reflection, on the anonymous photograph and the expressive self-portrait, have suggested a consistency in Ashbery's thinking about art in general, the impression ought to be deepened by a reading of "Wet Casements." I am not sure whether to call it a poem. Yet it has Ashbery's characteristic virtues of "wide authority and tact" and expounds what eighteenth-century critics used to call an original sentiment; so that, if one read it knowing nothing else of the author, one would want to call him a great writer of some sort. It is worth stopping at the epigraph to the poem, which comes from Kafka's "Wedding Preparations in the Country": "When Eduard Raban, coming along the passage, walked into the open doorway, he saw that it was raining. It was not raining much." The quotation ends there but, a page further on in the story, one finds a more revealing passage. Raban imagines recounting to some passerby the dull feverish unpleasantness of his existence, and says of himself: "So long as you say 'one' instead of 'I,' there's nothing in it and one can easily tell the story; but as soon as you admit to yourself that it is you yourself, you feel as though transfixed and are horrified." Kafka's is preeminently a story about the self-image of the hero and the way it is constituted by the fancied approval and disapproval he sees reflected in the faces of others. They may have seemed to Ashbery the same sort of others whom the poet just glimpsed as he fled from them in "Parergon," the people whom he deserted in order to meet them some day "under a better sky." Evidently, the poet's valor came from his indifference to their claim, whereas Raban's pathos comes from his submission to it.

Granting the distinction between Kafka's self in the story and Ashbery's in the poem, the distance that has to be passed in going from "one" to "I" still forms a common subject of both narratives. Yet the perplexity that Raban felt from being unknown and unremarked, the author of "Wet Casements" feels as much from being known and remarked:

> The conception is interesting: to see, as though reflected
> In streaming windowpanes, the look of others through
> Their own eyes. A digest of their correct impressions of
> Their self-analytical attitudes overlaid by your

Ghostly transparent face. You in falbalas
Of some distant but not too distant era, the cosmetics,
The shoes perfectly pointed, drifting (how long you
Have been drifting; how long I have too for that matter)
Like a bottle-imp toward a surface which can never be approached,
Never pierced through into the timeless energy of a present
Which would have its own opinions on these matters,
Are an epistemological snapshot of the processes
That first mentioned your name at some crowded cocktail
Party long ago, and someone (not the person addressed)
Overheard it and carried that name around in his wallet
For years as the wallet crumbled and bills slid in
And out of it. I want that information very much today,

Can't have it, and this makes me angry.
I shall use my anger to build a bridge like that
Of Avignon, on which people may dance for the feeling
Of dancing on a bridge. I shall at last see my complete face
Reflected not in the water but in the worn stone floor of my
        bridge.

I shall keep to myself.
I shall not repeat others' comments about me.

The poet shows no interest in the looks, impressions, and attitudes that he sketches, until he begins talking to himself, or to the aspect of himself represented by "your / Ghostly transparent face." By the time one comes to the phrase, "how long you / Have been drifting; how long I have too for that matter," one feels that his intimacy with "you" is all-important.

Ashbery said once that he thought of himself as John and the one who wrote his poems as Ashbery, and this made it interesting to hear at times what others were saying about Ashbery. John, I think, wrote this poem in defense of the fortunes of Ashbery's name. He had been a listener too often at parties where correct impressions of himself were overlaid by the self-analytical attitudes of others; had, like Whitman, heard himself "called by his nighest name" by those who were out of the game, which did not exist till they were out of it—a game that emerges from the mysterious enchantment of self with self. In response, he starts this new conversation with "you." But the motive that prompts it is his anger at learning that his name has been circulated—overheard, and picked up by someone it was not meant for—with the result that it took on the currency of rumor and not of fame. Two metaphors come so close together, in accounting for the reaction, that one cannot well distinguish between them, or between them and the name they are figures of. The metaphors evoke a piece of paper in a wallet and an old photograph. To retrieve the name by recovering these would mean to belong truly to one's experience, and at the same time to remain inseparably oneself. One cannot, however, do both. The name is irretrievable, and the poet builds his bridge from the recognition that things are so. People may dance there just for the feeling of dancing on a bridge; yet the place is his, all the same; for it bears the reflection of his face for him alone. I do not know whether Ashbery was conscious of revising the last lines of "Summer" in these last lines of "Wet Casements." But one cannot help placing the two endings side by side; and the revision shows a larger change of perspective. The reflection at last has become still more figurative than it was at first, and the poem has become as strange to the poet as it is to the others. His reward, such as it is, has to be surmised from the unhurried power of the final couplet, which with its two assertions joins in a single vow.

—David Bromwich, "John Ashbery: The Self Against Its Images," *Raritan* 4 (Spring 1986): 54–57.

KAREN MILLS-COURTS ON SEEKING THE SELF

[Karen Mills-Courts is a Professor of English at the State University of New York, Fredonia. She is the author of *Poetry as Epitaph: Representation and Poetic Language*, from which the following is extracted. Here, she characterizes Ashbery's work as a whole, and "Wet Casements" in particular, as a quest for self-discovery forever suspended just shy of completion.]

As David Kalstone has pointed out, this poet's work is certainly not autobiographical in any conventional or confessional sense of the word. Kalstone suggests, rather, that it is autobiography in the sense Wallace Stevens intended when he wrote that "it is often said of a man that his work is autobiographical in spite of every subterfuge. It cannot be otherwise ... even though it may be totally without reference to himself."[6] Kalstone is extremely perceptive here, as he is throughout his extraordinary essay on "Self-Portrait in a Convex Mirror." Ashbery, however, presses Kalstone's (and Stevens's) sense of autobiography to even further extremes: the poetry is intended not just as a record of the mind's activity but as an extension of the mind's living, as a "writing-into-existence" of the mind that acts. "I'm attempting to reproduce in poetry, the actions of a mind at work or rest," Ashbery has said.[7] The word *reproduce* is a long way from a diary-like notation. The distance becomes clearer as the poet expands his statement by discussing the relationship of music to his work: "the importance of music to me is that it takes time ... actually creates time as it goes along, or at any rate organizes it in a way that we can see or hear and it's something growing, which is another aspect of my poetry, I think; it's moving, growing, developing, I hope; that's what I want it to do anyway and these things take place in the framework of time" (*CP*, 120). This explains his proclivity for long poems where, he continues, "one is given much broader scope to work with and, as I said before, the time that it takes to write and the changes in one's mood and one's ideas enrich the texture of the poem considerably." The actual process of writing is "a continuing experience, an experience that continues to provide new reflections" (*CP*, 127). This revealing discussion of Ashbery's work culminates in his important final statement, which is about *Three Poems*:

> Somebody is being born; in other words at the end a person is somehow given an embodiment out of those proliferating reflections that are occurring in a generalized mind which eventually run together into the image of a specific person, "he" or "me," who was not there when the poem began. In "The System," I guess you might say that the person who has been born as "he" has taken over in the first person again and is continuing the debate. (*CP*, 131)

"Somebody is being born ... and is continuing the debate"—
Ashbery's need to keep writing in a state of active potential could
not be clearer. And it is also evident that he sees it as a self-
creation that occurs through the operations of language in time;
the self created instantly becomes a "he" through the proleptic
force of the "I." In Ashbery's "case," then, the work is
autobiographical in a much more radical sense than Stevens
suggests; it creates the "act of the mind" even as it records it. For
in "The System" the "I" rarely appears, and when it does it
quickly becomes another "he" left behind by the "I," who returns
in the first person only in "The Recital," which ends the whole
work. It is an "autobiography" that inherently rejects any
notation of a "personal life" and instead inscribes the "extreme
austerity of an almost empty mind." The embodiment of words
reveals the mind's quest for a fulfillment that it cannot afford to
find. Being alive is writing in a way that "actually creates time";
it is "continuing the debate," avoiding, even at the cost of clarity,
the "locking; into place" that is "death-itself."

Ashbery's acceptance of this radical temporality and constant
change is, however, only one part of his story. For it "provides
some bad moments," he says, "all links severed with the worldly
matrix from which it sprang, the soul feels that it is propelling
itself forward at an ever-increasing speed ... in the end the soul
cannot recognize itself and is as one lost, though it imagines it
has found eternal rest" (*TP*, 70–71). The lost self is one of
Ashbery's deepest concerns, and his desire for self-discovery
haunts, perhaps even motivates, all of his work. It is the ultimate
"nettle." We are, he believes, caught in a "colossal trick," which
has "filled up the whole universe" and is "roiling the clear waters
of reflective intellect, getting it into all kinds of messes that could
have been avoided if only, as Pascal says, we had the sense to stay
in our room" (*TP*, 56–57) The "trick" is that the "I" is constantly
drawn outside of itself, out of its "room," by a desire that only
seems to be a longing for all "other," for a "point" on the
landscape. It is really a desire *in* the self *for* the self. The trick is
productive, it has "filled up the whole universe," but it sends
consciousness on a fool's journey: the "individual will ... sallies

forth full of ardor and hubris, bent on self-discovery in the guise of an attractive partner" (*TP*, 57). The self who "sallies forth" in desire looks in the wrong direction, has its "eyes averted from the truth," but there is no alternative since its "truth" is only the emptiness of its own desire for meaning. The misdirected journey creates a situation in which one cannot find "the reflection of one's own face" because "true reflective thinking has been annihilated." The denial of self-reflection is, however, the creation of life-itself, the "universal task" (*TP*, 57–58). Performing this life-creating task cannot alleviate the desire that lives by virtue of its performance: the end of desire is the end of life.

One remains, then, "bent on self-discovery" while traveling all the detours set up by the "colossal trick" of having to look outward rather than inward, forward rather than backward. "Propelling itself forward" is the only option of the living "I":

> if backward looks were possible, not nostalgia
> but a series of carefully selected views, hieratic
> as icons, the difficulty would be eased and self
> could merge with selflessness, in a true apprecia-
> tion of the tremendous volumes of eternity. But this
> is impossible ... it can only result in destruction
> and even death.
>
> (*TP*, 71)

Truly a form of differance, Ashbery's consciousness differs from its own past, longs for a full presence that a "merging" with that past would offer, and defers "merging" as in avoidance of "destruction and even death." Like Derrida, Ashbery understands this desire for presence as "nostalgia" and yet, even though he rejects nostalgia, he cannot prevent the longing for some sort of self-representation that might provide self-presence. The lost soul cries out for recognition, "cannot recognize itself" in its representations, and continues to seek some form of embodiment that does not kill. In this moment, the poet suggests that such a form would be an "icon," a sacred representation that attains its sanctity by virtue of its ability to "embody" a living presence that is elsewhere. An icon might mediate between the past self and its lost "god." To establish such a figure, however, the poet would have to be able to discern which moment of his past contains a significance so primary that it can institute itself as an "iconic" moment. Such a "hieratic" view is impossible for a poet whose past seems to be distributed as equally significant (car insignificant) particles, as fragments. Without "backward looks" one cannot identify the particular fragment of one's self that would bestow full being. One is left only with "nostalgia," which always marks the loss of the past, not its restoration. It is not surprising that "the other side of nostalgia" evokes in Ashbery the gesture that Derrida attributes to Heidegger, a seeking for the "right words." Even this poet who characterizes himself as a "disabused intellect" (*TP*, 112), who knows that self-presence is death, remains "bent on self-discovery" and thereby participates in his own version of "Heideggerean hope."

> *You know now the sorrow of continually doing*
> *something that you cannot name, or producing*
> *automatically, as an apple tree produces*
> *apples, this thing there is no name for.*
> —John Ashbery, *Three Poems*

Ashbery's "hope that doesn't take itself seriously" is, in spite of his typically casual phrasing, complicated and powerful. In that hope lies every possibility for exploring the great question that initiates all others, the question that "revolves around you, your being here" (*TP*, 151). The self, exploring its own being, can hope for the self-discovery on which it is "bent" only through the otherness of words. Words are the "attractive others" which can bridge the trap between the poet and those equally attractive "points," the "landscape" he "wants" and to which he wants to "communicate / Something between breaths." The words and the other "points" are all implicated in the poet's endlessly detoured drive toward self-presence, a drive that must produce poetry in which "flexing is its account," where words operate in such a way that they avoid the tomb-like freezing, the immobility, of a "diary." For crucial to the project of self-discovery is "the opportunity of definitively clearing your name"

(*TP*, 51). Yet that "clearing," that exposure of the "I," cannot be carved into a clarity that suggests any finality, an end to "moving, growing, developing." The clearing must not occur as "mummified writing" ("Litany," *AWK*, 8, 23, 68). The discovery of a cleared name, while much desired, offers its own sort of dangers, though the seeking of that name provides the basis of his poetry. Ashbery considers the problem explicitly in "Wet Casements," a poem "about" seeking the self through the other. "The conception is interesting," he says,

> to see as though reflected
> In streaming windowpanes, the look of others through
> Their self-analytical attitudes overlaid by your
> Ghostly transparent face.
>
> (*HD*, 28)

"The look of others," projected through an openness that is vulnerable to the changes of the weather—projected, that is, through "wet casements"—is always "the others'" attempt at self-discovery, their own "self-analytical attitudes." Thus, one's own face, reflected through their eyes, is reduced to a "ghostly transparent face," a face through which that look may *pass* as it attempts to return to its "point of no return." Such a process inevitably makes the "I" into a "you" and leaves both aspects of the self "drifting," "like a bottle-imp toward a surface which can never be approached, / Never pierced through into the timeless energy of a present" (*HD*, 28). The process will have "mentioned your name" as it was happening, the poet continues, but the passing reference is immediately lost as the name, only "overheard," is "carried away like an "epistemological snapshot" in a stranger's "wallet." When one realizes that the lost name is only a "snapshot" of the reflective process, not even of the poet's face, the extent of the loss is so complete that it is obvious that the name is utterly beyond retrieval. In the midst of this recognition, the poet discovers a passion much more intense than his initial "interest." Drifting as only a ghostly face and an "overheard" but lost name, he wants to find the name in order to "complete" himself

I want that information very much today,
Can't have it, and this makes me angry
I shall use my anger to build a bridge like that
Of Avignon, on which people may dance for the feeling
Of dancing on a bridge. I shall at last see my complete face
Reflected not in the water but in the worn stone floor of my
    bridge

(HD, 28)

The important point here is that the hunger for one's own name is what generates the bridge of poetry. It is a hunger for the self which cannot be satisfied by the eyes of others who only abscond with the name in their own "bent toward self-discovery," and it is a hunger, finally, that cannot be satisfied in life. "This thing there is no name for," both the "I" and the poetry it produces, can achieve presence only "at last," and even then it does not find its name or its face but only its image: "my complete face / Reflected." And as always in Ashbery that "complete" reflection will not be found in the moving waters that suggest life and refer to the "wet casements," but in the "death" of the completed "stone floor." "At last"—when the bridge of words between the self and others is no longer "flexing" but finished—"I shall keep to myself," the poet writes with his usual gentle irony, "I shall not repeat others' words about me." His irony resides in the fact that such a future "at last" is a projected end to the "interesting" process, which is literally a process of "conception," as he has said in his opening line. It is the only sort of "birth" that the "I" can know: self-conception through a projection into "the look of others." When one keeps to oneself, ends the repetition of desire, no longer repeats "others' comments," life, as well as the poetic bridge, is finished. At that point words become "a permanent medium in which we are lost."

NOTES

6. David Kalstone, "John Ashbery: Self-Portrait in a Convex Mirror," in *Five Temperaments* (New York, 1977), 171. Kalstone's essay offers an excellent "reading, lesson," a lesson in how to approach Ashbery's work. His

understanding of Ashbery's work as process rather than as product, his sensitivity to the motivations and meanings of Self-Portrait, and his excellent discussion of the autobiographical elements of poetry in general have enriched my own responses to this poet.

—Karen Mills-Courts, *Poetry as Epitaph: Representation and Poetic Language* (Baton Rouge: Lousiana State University Press, 1990): 279–284.

JOHN SHOPTAW ON A BRIDGE STILL UNDER CONSTRUCTION

[John Shoptaw is a critic, poet, and author of numerous articles on Ashbery. He has taught courses on poetry and literature at Princeton and Yale. This extract from his full-length study of Ashbery's poetry (*Some Trees* through *Flow Chart*) provides some background on the writing of the poem and a grammatical basis for a qualified reading of the concluding couplet.]

One of Ashbery's finest anti-confessional poems, "Wet Casements" (HBD 28; dated March 22, 1975), grew out of an embarrassing and frustrating experience. A poet paid the newly famous Ashbery a visit: "He began asking questions that I found very deep and almost painful to contemplate. This strange transformation interested me very much. At one point it was almost as if we were seeing ourselves in each other. I was looking at him but it seemed as though I was looking at myself. He pointed out this phenomenon."[12] Ashbery found an analogy for this experience in Kafka's unfinished story, "Wedding Preparations in the Country" which provided him with his epigraph: "When Eduard Raban, coming along the passage, walked into the open doorway, he saw that it was raining. It was not raining much." What interests Ashbery here is the device narrative theorists call focalization: the reader views Raban's view of the rain: "It was not raining much." This voyeuristic "look of others through / Their own eyes" becomes uncomfortable when the look, with its own point of view, turns on oneself. Another passage from Kafka's story describes something like Ashbery's experience with the visiting poet. Raban notices a woman looking at him:

> She did so indifferently, and she was perhaps, in any case, only looking at the falling rain in front of him.... Raban thought she looked amazed. "Well," he thought...... One works so feverishly at the office that afterwards one is too tired even to enjoy one's holidays properly. But even all that work does not give one a claim to be treated lovingly by everyone; on the contrary, one is alone, a total stranger and only an object of curiosity. And so long as you say 'one' instead of 'I,' there's nothing in it and one can easily tell the story; but as soon as you admit to yourself that it is you yourself, you feel as though transfixed and are horrified."[13]

The narrative deflection of the gaze onto a generalizing pronoun or a character's name is costly: it divides "I" from "myself," consciousness from self-consciousness. Their wedding preparations never end.

In "Wet Casements" the troubling interdependence of one upon others and upon oneself is inescapable. But the tearful "streaming windowpanes" show how painful objectification can be.[14] The misrepresentation of Ashbery in his readers' "digest of their correct impressions" of him is as alienating as it is "interesting." Ashbery already felt the splitting of his published from his private personality in "Worsening Situation": "This severed hand" that writes "is ever / A stranger who walks beside me." Efforts at the reintegration of one's self, at the repossession of one's name, sound hysterical: "The name you drop and never say is mine, mine!" (SP 3). The author here promises "Some day I'll claim to you how all used up / I am because of you" (SP 3), and "Wet Casements" keeps that promise. The poem is measured into dwindling sentences and three shrinking stanzas. The first and longest stanza consists of a series of appositional clauses and sentences revolving around "you." Its nuclear argument runs as follows: It is interesting to see the look of others at oneself, a digest of their impressions; "You" are the result ("snapshot") of your name being circulated. With an elongated, drugged sentence, "You in falbalas / ... the cosmetics, / The shoes perfectly pointed," the poet (ad)dresses himself in the second person. But the submerged sensual drift exceeds simple negation. "You" is also powerfully attracted toward its narcissistic image: "Like a bottle-imp toward a surface which can never be approached, / Never pierced through." Whether or not one is alone, the hymeneal mirror surface remains unbroken. The "bottle-imp" is a scientific toy consisting of a hollow figure in a column of water, which responds to varying pressure by rising, plunging, and remaining in suspension. Its other name, the Cartesian devil, brings Descartes's reflective cogito into Ashbery's picture.[15] Our composite "Ashbery" is "an epistemological snapshot" of associations: New York School experimentalist, important writer, difficult poet, and so forth. In the literary market his famed "name circulates," a loaded phrase in which the name is already recognized as cultural capital: "someone" picked up the name dropped "and carried that name around in his wallet / For years as the wallet crumbled and bills slid in / And out of it" ("wall," "Bill"). One's name is also subject to deterioration.

The first stanza of "Wet Casements" does not break after that simile, as we would expect, but after an incomplete sentence: "I want that information very much today, / / Can't have it, and this makes me angry." The desire to recover one's name cannot be realized. Ashbery's frustration, now in the first person, produces another desire and a beautiful complex image, a Pauline mirror-bridge: "I shall at last see my complete face / Reflected not in the water but in the worn stone floor of my bridge." Ashbery's poetry is his communication bridge, which includes both himself and his circle of readers, joined in a round dance ("sur le pont d'Avignon on y danse, on y danse"). The bridge, "worn" like a costume or billfold, reconstructs, with Crane's assistance, Whitman's "Crossing Brooklyn Ferry" Whitman too imagined "the look of others": "Just as you feel when you look on the river and sky, so I felt" (309), a syntax mirrored in "Wet Casements": "(how long you / Have been drifting; how long I have too for that matter)." Whitman's image returns to him not through a glass darkly but face to face: "Flood-tide below me! I see you face to face!" (307). But Ashbery's reflection is still partial. Like Kafka's story and the middle stanza of "Wet Casements," the bridge at Avignon is incomplete. The Pauline prophecy remains unfulfilled because communication is still under construction.

Yet the closing stanzaic couplet seems perfectly self-contained: "I shall keep to myself. / I shall not repeat others' comments about me." Harold Bloom praises this stanza for its "sermon-like directness."[16] It is true that the "I want" of the first stanza yields to four prophecies beginning "I shall." But the self-commandments of the last stanza are marked discursively as a journal entry. Even in these published private resolutions to keep oneself and one's name private, oneself is two: two lines and sentences each with "I" on one end mirroring its reflective object, "myself" and "me," on the other. Privacy, Ashbery realizes, can be no healing alternative to publicity. The mirrors of other people, however distorted and reductive, are the only looking-glasses around.

NOTES

12. Remnick, unpublished interview, 17.

13. Franz Kafka, *The Complete Stories*, ed. Nahum N. Glatzer (New York: Schocken, 1976) 53.

14. These casements may be related to the fact that Ashbery began wearing glasses around this time.

15. For another likely source of Ashbery's "bottle-imp" (first called "ludion"), see Roussel, *Locus Solus*, trans. Rupert Copeland Cunningham (New York: Riverrun, 1983) 51–92.

16. Harold Bloom, "Measuring the Canon: John Ashbery's *Wet Casements* and *Tapestry*," *Agon: Towards a Theory of Revisionism* (New York: Oxford UP, 1982) 283. See also David Bromwich, "John Ashbery," *Raritan* 4 (Spring 1986): 54–57.

—John Shoptaw, *On the Outside Looking Out* (Cambridge: Harvard Univ. Press, 1994): 199–201.

CRITICAL ANALYSIS OF

"Syringa"

Unlike some allusions in Ashbery's verse, which can be overlooked without robbing a poem of its meaning, the myth of Orpheus and Eurydice is critical to making sense of "Syringa." Briefly, Orpheus, mortal son of Apollo, was a famed poet and musician who played so well on a lyre given to him by his father that he was able to charm wild beasts and make trees and rocks dance. One day Orpheus met Eurydice and fell deeply in love, but alas, Eurydice stepped on a serpent, was killed, and descended to the underworld. Unwilling to let go, Orpheus played and sang his way into the nether regions and convinced the powers that be to let him retrieve Eurydice, on one condition: that he advance ahead of her and never look back until they emerged topside. Unfortunately, Orpheus's desire and nostalgia got the best of him; he looked back just as they were almost home free and Eurydice faded back into death's domain. Accounts differ on what happened after that—some feature a reunion after Orpheus is dismembered by Thracian women in the throes of Bacchic ecstasy, hence the line in the poem, "Orpheus realized this / And didn't mind so much about his reward being in heaven / After the Bacchantes had torn him apart"—but the myth is generally understood as an allegory about the power of art and the folly of regret. Orpheus, of course, became the archetypal poet and musician, around whom a mystery cult was formed in ancient times and to whose story countless poems, paintings, and compositions have alluded ever since.

In "Syringa," Ashbery plays with the myth in a number of ways. Most explicit is his positioning of Orpheus on one side of an internal deliberation over the function of art and futility of nostalgia. In Ashbery's formulation, Orpheus represents the desire to resurrect or keep alive the memory of what was lost, most often expressed in elegies and other artistic forms that hearken back to the past for added aesthetic weight. In opposition to this is Ashbery's innovative experimentation with form and distinctive tendency to focus on the present as the source of poetic inspiration—his desire to represent, as he once put it, "they way time feels *as it passes*" (my emphasis). Lines supporting this viewpoint include 13-21 (beginning with "But it is the nature of things"), lines 41-43 ("For although memories, of a season..."), as well as the succinct opening lines of the second verse paragraph ("But how late to be regretting all this, even / Bearing in mind that regrets are always late, too late!"). Further embodying this idea is the somewhat buried meaning of the poem's title. According to Webster's Unabridged Dictionary, "Syringa" is a botanical term for "any shrub of the genus *Philadelphus*, certain species of which are cultivated as ornamentals." Although it is possible Ashbery is referring to the "flowing, fleeting" nature of flowers in bloom, enjoyed in the moment but impossible to capture forever, a much more likely reason for entitling the poem "Syringa" lies in the word's etymological roots. In ancient Greek and Latin, Syringa is the accusative case of Syrinx, another figure from classical mythology, whose fellow river nymphs changed her into a reed to save her from Pan's lascivious advances. In Ovid's recounting (almost certainly read by Ashbery at Harvard), Pan lunges for Syrinx right at the moment of her transformation and his breath blows over the reeds she becomes, making a sound like moaning. Intrigued, Pan cuts a few of the reeds and fashions his trademark "panpipe." Thus we have another myth in which music (and by extension, art in general) becomes a tool for recovering a lost object of affection. The critical importance of Ashbery's invocation of "Syringa" lies in the fact that she is the other side of the equation—she is what was lost in the process of memorializing. On a reed by the riverside, the mere blowing of air makes another kind of music—a music of the moment, un-composed and ego-less. When Pan cuts the reeds, he fashions Syringa into an instrument for his own gratification, however much he thinks he is preserving her legacy. The accusative "Syringa" is transformed into the nominative "Syrinx" (which is also the Greek word for panpipe). Ashbery's decision to use as his title the obscure, accusative variation of the nymph's name over her more commonly known one syntactically emphasizes this theme of sublimation that turns a life, a myth, a work of art into the passive instrument of another time, another place. The theme is also reinforced textually—beyond the titular clue, the only allusions within the poem to Syrinx/Syringa are indirect ("the tossing reeds of that slow, / Powerful stream" and, less definitely, the "tiny, sparkling yellow flowers"). The nymph has thus morphed from animate being to plant, from plant to inanimate instrument, from instrument to myth, and from myth to an underlying concept in a poem. The complexity and pathos of "Syringa" lies in its attempt to decry this process while inexorably participating in it.

Compounding this conceptual tension is the speaker's somewhat defensive need to forget the past, which seems to mask an actual loss on the poet's part and the resultant attempt to distract himself from a painful memory with purely rhetorical talk. This emotional distancing allows him to arrive at some objective observations about the mind's habit of assessing the past and the limitations of an artist on the longevity and cultural import of their creations. Ruefully quoting Shakespeare ("The end crowns all"), chief god in the pantheon of writers, he decides that only in retrospect is it possible to make value judgments ("say it is good or bad"). Likewise, "stellification" (the ultimate ego objective of any artist) "is for the few, and comes much later." In this sense, the trajectory of an artwork is dictated by unknown and uncontrollable forces, and something highly personal becomes "a bad / Comet screaming hate and disaster, but so turned inward / That the meaning, good or other, can never / Become known."

At least not known to the poet, whose fate it is to "disappear into libraries, onto microfilm" until some "arbitrary chorus / Speaks of a totally different incident with a similar name" and, like Pan, fashions a new use for him. Thus the poem concludes on a bittersweet note; resigned to the impossibility of preserving the past or controlling the future, the modern poet can do little else but focus on the present. And to the challenge, "why pick at a dull pavan few care / to Follow" (a pavan is kind of archaic, courtly dance), the poet can only reply, "But why not?"

"Syringa"

RICHARD JACKSON ON DECONSTRUCTING ASHBERY

[Richard Jackson is a UC Foundation Professor of English at the University of Tennessee, Chattanooga and an award-winning poet. In addition to recent poetry collections (*Heartwall* and *Alive All Day*), he is the author of *Dismantling Time in Contemporary Poetry*. In the following extract, he endeavors to show how Ashbery's poetry, and "Syringa" in particular, embodies the deconstructionist theories of Derrida and Foucault.]

It should not surprise us that one of John Ashbery's new poems, "Drame Bourgeois," was first published as an epigraphic coda to a recent issue of *Yale French Studies* entitled *Graphesis* (the title word a neologism that does work similar to that of "deconstruction" as employed by Jacques Derrida and Michel Foucault), an issue which explored the relation between philosophic and literary discourse. Earlier in his career, of course, Ashbery published some French poems in the review *Tel Quel*, a meeting place for writers like Foucault and Derrida, as well as Roland Barthes and others—and it is this French connection rather than the usual analogies to painting that best explains Ashbery's work.

"Drame Bourgeois" is concerned with the peculiar nature of writing as such—with books as opposed to speech. Writing occurs where the "Moment of outline recedes / ... always darker as the vanishing point / Is turned and turns itself / Into an old army blanket, or something flat and material." As the editor of *Yale French Studies* points out, the poem "talks about the non-referentiality of the imaginary process: objects are turned into ideas and can be grasped only at the limit of some 'non-real' border line or 'vanishing point.'" The experience of poetry at Ashbery's "vanishing point" is what Foucault calls the act of "transgression":

the moment when language, arriving at its confines, overleaps itself, explodes and radically challenges itself ... and where it remains fixed in this way at the limit of its void, speaking of itself in a second language in which the absence of a sovereign subject outlines its essential emptiness and incessantly fractures the unity of its discourse.

("Preface to Transgression" in *Language, Counter-Memory, Practice*)

It should be added that the vanishing point, the scene of transgression, is writing itself, the bare word "flat and material" on the page, isolated, as Derrida says, from the author's intentions, free to begin its own disconcerting and pluralistic enterprise. The result of this emptying process for the poet is a turning away from the "too bright" blaze of his own volumes, a relinquishing of the traditional author's authority, a cutting loose from the intention to "mean" something final:

Your very lack of information is special to me,
Your emptying glance, prisms which I treasure up.
Only let your voice not become this clarion,
Alarum in the wilderness, calling me back to piety, to sense,
Else I am undone, for late haze rapes the golf links
And the gilded spines of these tomes blaze too bright.

All writing leads towards the detachment of the library, towards the "second language" that Ashbery so often characterizes not by definite hues or depths of meaning, but by its brilliant surface, the prism or spectrum of *possible* colors. (...)

Is there any history possible for this poetry of decentered moments? In his essay "Nietzsche, Genealogy, History" (*Language, Counter-Memory, Practice*), Foucault notes that the process of decentering or deconstructing is effected by a Nietzschean genealogy that is concerned with the provisional rather than final structure of events. By its refusal to focus on major events that establish continuous, stable patterns, and its patient attention to singular details, no matter how disruptive or discontinuous with each other, genealogy establishes a "counter-memory—a transformation of history into a totally different form of time." Now Ashbery's "Pyrography" exactly describes such a genealogical approach, and as such a description, signals Ashbery's abandonment of his earlier "leaving out business" that marked his first few books. This poem reconsiders the ideological and cultural history of nineteenth-century America's westward movement and its present after-effects. The aim is to deconstruct our myth of completion, our sense of having constructed an edifice in which to center ourselves. Ashbery's analysis uncovers a different structure that poses an opposite view of our situation:

> How are we to inhabit
> This space from which the fourth wall is invariably missing,
> As in a stage-set or dollhouse, except by staying as we are,
> In lost profile, facing the stars, with dozens of as yet
> Unrealized projects, and a strict sense
> Of time running out, of evening presenting
> The tactfully folded over bill?

The answer is provided by a genealogy itself and lies in the very structure of deferral it produces by its "vast unravelling" that extends indefinitely towards "the darkness beyond"—towards what is always absent:

> if we were going
> To be able to write the history of our time, starting with today,
> It would be necessary to model all these unimportant details ....
> And not just the major events but the whole incredible
> Mass of everything happening simultaneously and pairing off,
> Channeling itself into history.

In this scheme history becomes a narrative constantly altered—*rewritten*—as new events subvert, rupture our provisional structures for it. Narrative structure does not imitate our received traditions, but becomes the creator, the catalyst of new possibilities.

What becomes of the poet in such a complex history? As Ashbery says in the penultimate poem, "Syringa," which powerfully embodies Foucault's main theories, the poet must "forget" the Orphic desire to dwell upon repetitions, upon the lost presence of his Eurydice. He must realize that it is "the nature of things to be seen only once" in their uniqueness, that he cannot "treasure / That stalled moment. It is too flowing, fleeting." He must realize that his subject is soon "no longer / Material for a poem" for any subject as such is too intent upon revealing a stable meaning,

> While the poem streaked by, its tail afire, a bad
> Comet screaming hate and disaster, but so turned inward
> That the meaning, good or other, can never
> Become known.

But this is not solipsism. The poet must realize that he too must cut himself off from the poem, that he, like it, must disappear at the "vanishing point" as both become part of what Foucault calls the "library," the "archive," to be subject to later archeologies. The author, man ultimately, "disappears" in the sense that he is no longer the central issue. He becomes literally the text's *rebus*, the meaning of whose hidden syllables is deferred towards an indefinite future, an absence, a *differance*. I quote from the last lines of this poem:

> The singer thinks
> Constructively, builds up his chant in progressive stages
> Like a skyscraper, but at the last minute turns away.
> The song is engulfed in an instant in blackness
> Which must in turn flood the whole continent
> With blackness, for it cannot see. The singer
> Must then pass out of sight, not even relieved
> Of the evil burthen of the words. Stellification
> Is for the few, and comes about much later
> When all record of these people and their lives
> Has disappeared into libraries, onto microfilm.
> A few are still interested in them. "But what about
> So-and-so?" is still asked on occasion. But they lie
> Frozen and out of touch until an arbitrary chorus
> Speaks of a totally different incident with a similar name
> In whose tale are hidden syllables

Of what happened so long before that
In some small town, one indifferent summer.

The result is not, as critics of Foucault or Ashbery suggest, a meaningless end to the history of man, but rather a new freedom of the poet, of man, to continue to begin, to transgress the limits of language, to continue to decenter himself to accommodate the exigencies of the moment. And it is a new freedom for readers, too. It is perhaps our "arbitrary chorus" as critics and as poets which retrieves texts from the "archive" though it may be a chorus that "Speaks of a totally different incident with a similar name." Though hidden in the archive, the poem can, when uncovered, provide for the play of infinite possibilities; this is both the difficulty and high promise of *Houseboat Days*, a book which is, in short, a profound analysis of the rhetoric that constitutes our temporality. The book rests squarely in the archive projected by Shelley in his *Defence*: "All high poetry is infinite; it is as the first acorn, which contained all oaks potentially. Veil after veil may be undrawn ..., and after one person of one age has exhausted all its divine effluence which their peculiar relations enable them to share, another and yet another succeeds, and new relations are ever developed."

—Richard Jackson, "Writing as Transgression: Ashbery's Archeology of the Moment," *Southern Humanities Review* 12:3 (Summer 1978): 279–280; 282–284.

LAWRENCE KRAMER ON THE TWO VOICES OF ASHBERY

[Lawrence Kramer is a Professor of English and Music at Fordham University. The author of six books (including *Music and Poetry* and *Music and Meaning*) and numerous articles, Kramer is also co-editor of the journal *19th Century Music*. Kramer's essay on Elliot Carter's musical adaptation of the poem contains a cogent explanation of the poem's polyvocal tension, the gist of which is extracted here.]

Ashbery's "Syringa" is a series of reflections on the Orpheus myth. Its burden, as so often in Ashbery's work, is loss, a loss that makes three demands: first, that it must be represented poetically; second, that it must be represented with reticence; and third, that it must be represented without evasion. Many of Ashbery's poems can be understood as solutions to the problem of reconciling these obviously antagonistic demands, and "Syringa" is one of them. Its solution is to use Orpheus's loss of Eurydice as a deliberately unsubtle metaphor for a personal loss of the speaker's, at the same time as it declines ever to identify the speaker's loss or even to allude to it until the poem ends, at which point the personal loss is "no longer / Material for a poem." The effect of this is slightly dizzying. Someone who meditates on Orpheus's loss to escape the burden of his own loss is actually just pretending to meditate on Orpheus. The speaker in Ashbery's poem, however, is *not* pretending that: he is only *pretending* to pretend it. The personal loss is an open secret; the tale of Orpheus that hides its identity is also an exposure of its presence. As a result, the speaker's refusal to refer to his own loss does not seem evasive; it seems ascetic, as if he were constructing an elegy while refusing himself the implicit consolations of personal pathos—praise, memory, understanding. At the same time, Orpheus's loss becomes a topic of authentic concern in the poem, not just a pretext. The poem is, in effect, polyvocal. It has a meditative voice that engages in a tranquil, resigned consideration of the problem of loss as presented by Orpheus, and it has an elegaic voice, full of lament and desire, that uses the Orpheus myth to utter "hidden syllables" of personal sorrow.

These two voices are always moving in opposite directions. The elegaic voice, which is to some degree the voice of Orpheus himself, is always retrospective, always "coming back / To the mooring of starting out" ("Soonest Mended," *DD*, p. 19), the lost past. Against this, the meditative voice poses a refusal to overinvest the self in the "stalled moment" of remembered happiness. Whereas the elegaic voice resists the passing of time, the meditative voice seeks to consent to time's every motion, to ask for nothing more than the "flowing" and "fleeting." Against an Orphean time, it sets a Heraclitean one. Despite this divergence, however; the two voices of the poem are tightly woven together. In fact, there is no moment in "Syringa" when either voice sounds apart from the other; both are simultaneously present throughout. The conventional way to put this would be to say that throughout the poem the speaker is ambivalent; but that is precisely how I would prefer not to put it. Ambivalence implies conflict; the poem discloses none. Its feeling tone is a unity, a singularity; but it is polyvocal. Its two voices compose only one utterance, just as, say, Carter's *Third Quartet* is itself not a pair of duos but music polyvocally *composed* of two duos.

The details of how Ashbery accomplishes his polyvocal form will emerge gradually. For the moment, its projection in Carter's "Syringa" can be described. "Syringa" is composed for mezzo-soprano, bass, and chamber ensemble. The mezzo takes on the role of the poem's meditative voice, and it is she who sings the text of Ashbery's "Syringa." Her music is simple, graceful, and generally quiet. Articulating each word of text with great clarity, it evokes a mood of lucidity and contemplation. At the same time, passing through the text without repetition or embellishment, the mezzo line embodies the consent to the passing of time that is the poem's central meditative attitude. The mezzo's polyvocal partner is, of course, the bass. Singing simultaneously with the mezzo and independent of her, the bass provides the poem's Orphean voice, filling in what Carter describes as the "subliminal background that might be evoked in the mind of a reader" of Ashbery's text.[2] The bass sings, in ancient Greek, an agitated, complex, mournful part, one that sometimes suggests archaic, melismatic vocal styles. With his passionate chanting, lingering over the dead in a dead language—the dead's language?—the bass suggests the will to lament, the exaltation of regret, that characterizes Orpheus in the poem and that constitutes, in the meditative voice's view, his "mistake."

In traditional music, these two voices might be opposed to each other through contrastive statements and developments, just as in traditional poetry (Tennyson's "The Two Voices," for example) they would enter into an antiphonal argument. Overlapped, or "layered," as they are in the two "Syringa" texts, the voices are not *opposed* to each other at all, but *posed against* each other. Each remains perfectly distinct; yet the two together form a singularity, a kind of third voice, that is the integral voice of "Syringa"—the voice one hears in how the music sounds, how the poem reads. Carter underscores the radical oneness of this voice by bringing its constituent voices together at crucial moments by means of bilingual puns, several of which Andrew Porter points out in his *New Yorker* notice of the premiere of "Syringa."[3] The most important of these comes at the end of the piece, where the mezzo intones the poem's last word, "summer," while the bass sings "*soma, sema*" (body, tomb). This rapprochement of the voices is particularly poignant because it occurs as, simultaneously, the meditative voice approaches lament at last and the Orphean voice surrenders lament in exhaustion. Each voice, in other words, takes on the other's role as a way of falling silent, of finding relief from "the evil burthen of the words" (*HD*, p. 71). In the poem, the same thing happens when the meditative voice at last acknowledges that its own loss constitutes a reanimation of the Orpheus myth, "In whose tale are hidden syllables / Of what happened ... / In some small town, one indifferent summer" (*HD*, p. 71). Here, in its one act of personal memory, the meditative voice accepts the identity with Orpheus that it has so far left to its polyvocal partner. Yet at the same time it forecloses all further lament by stopping the poem.

NOTES

2. Program notes to the premiere of "Syringa," December 11, 1978.
3. "Famous Orpheus," *New Yorker* 54, no. 47 (January 8, 1979): 56–62.

—Lawrence Kramer, "'Syringa': John Ashbery and Elliot Carter," *Beyond Amazement: New Essays on John Ashbery*, ed. David Lehman (Ithaca: Cornell University Press, 1980): 256–259.

DAVID BROMWICH ON KNOWLEDGE'S BELATED ARRIVAL

[In an extract from an earlier section of his *Raritan* essay, Bromwich interprets "Syringa" as a perfect embodiment of the Ashberyan paradox whereby epiphanies afforded by art always occur too late to adapt them to life.]

What has love to do with the writing of poetry? Ashbery comes close to an answer in the concluding lines of "Street Musicians," which compare the memory of any action or passion to an inscription on the landscape, a deposit with a signature that happens to be ours.

> Our question of a place of origin hangs
> Like smoke: how we picnicked in pine forests,
> In coves with the water always seeping up, and left
> Our trash, sperm and excrement everywhere, smeared
> On the landscape, to make of us what we could.

So to the question, What did our love make of us? the poet has to reply: not what we wished; only a deformation, which we cherish anyway. Still, writing has an advantage over unassisted memory. It slows down the processes of annihilation by placing a small monument in their path—indeed, this is the motive of "Street Musicians," which begins with the report of a death. Also, unlike experience, it has a pathos that changes slightly at times, as its feelings move from person to person. These features help it to survive, and to commemorate a way of life that may have lacked a name till then.

The poet's tone of complicity implies that his elegies belong to all of us. But who are we? People who start to call a thing "life" once we know that we care for it. By contrast, the poet is someone who keeps thinking about the commonness and even the sordidness of the thing we chose. His attachment to this unnatural work makes him an exile from us; and he elects as a companion someone named you. Placed beside the latter personage, we look no different from "the others." Such have been the premises of Ashbery's poems, from *The Double Dream of Spring* on—conventions so familiar by now that it feels pedantic to rehearse them. It remains a puzzle why the game of pretended solidarity and genuine concealment should occur as steadily as it does in his writing, which allows few things to happen twice. But Ashbery has gone far to explain it in "Syringa," with a patient eloquence and a depth of allegorical detail that make the poem worth quoting at length.

Orpheus liked the glad personal quality
Of the things beneath the sky. Of course, Eurydice was a part
Of this. Then one day, everything changed. He rends
Rocks into fissures with lament. Gullies, hummocks
Can't withstand it. The sky shudders from one horizon
To the other, almost ready to give up wholeness.
Then Apollo quietly told him: "Leave it all on earth.
Your lute, what point? Why pick at a dull pavan few care to
Follow, except a few birds of dusty feather,
Not vivid performances of the past." But why not?
All other things must change too.
The seasons are no longer what they once were,
But it is the nature of things to be seen only once,
As they happen along, bumping into other things, getting along
Somehow. That's where Orpheus made his mistake.
Of course Eurydice vanished into the shade;
She would have even if he hadn't turned around.
No use standing there like a gray stone toga as the whole wheel
Of recorded history flashes past, struck dumb, unable to utter
    an intelligent
Comment on the most thought-provoking element in its train.
Only love stays on the brain, and something these people,
These other ones, call life. Singing accurately
So that the notes mount straight up out of the well of
Dim noon and rival the tiny, sparkling yellow flowers
Growing around the brink of the quarry, encapsulizes
The different weights of things.
                                    But it isn't enough
To just go on singing. Orpheus realized this
And didn't mind so much about his reward being in heaven
After the Bacchantes had torn him apart, driven
Half out of their minds by his music, what it was doing to them.
Some say it was for his treatment of Eurydice.
But probably the music had more to do with it, and
The way music passes, emblematic
Of life and how you cannot isolate a note of it
And say it is good or bad.

Orpheus, first of poets, likes the "glad personal quality / Of the things beneath the sky," and he naturally assumes his poetry will bring them closer. If it did so, it would cooperate with his need for ordinary companionship and also for love: "Of course, Eurydice was a part / Of this." But the poem means to disappoint any hope that poetry can redeem these things.

As the plot advances, one comes to see that Eurydice's loss was a necessary condition of the power of Orpheus's music. The comic feeling with which Ashbery invests this catastrophe is partly owing to the good-natured pessimism of Apollo's challenge. A healer and prosodist whose laws of balance Orpheus has broken, he speaks for the monuments of the past against the genius of the present, and the drama of the entire poem follows from Orpheus's silence here. It is Ashbery who speaks for him: "But why not? / All other things must change too." Harold Rosenberg wrote of "art's aim of changing the landscape," and for Ashbery this conception must never be allowed to relax into a mere figure of speech. The effects of Orpheus's song are accordingly described in a present tense that would suit an epic hero: "He rends / Rocks into fissures with lament." Heroic as it may be, such language offers a view of art's influence on life that is not therapeutic or even ameliorative. If, to pursue Rosenberg's aphorisms a step further, "the Rocky Mountains have resembled fake art for over a century," the solution is to change it all on earth. Alter the position of the trees, the mountains, the creatures, by enchanting them with music, so that they come nearer just for the sake of listening. This renewal of the present, however, is accomplished not only by the loss of Eurydice, but by the expulsion from the poet of any sense of his effect or his reward. Moralists have their own explanation of his fate—"Some say it was for his treatment of Eurydice"—but readers and listeners feel otherwise: "probably the music had more to do with it, and / The way music passes." In proportion, therefore, as Orpheus sang accurately, his notes will have been scattered with a reach and pattern that looks like the result of aimlessness.

So far, we have a picture of the artist as a person so receptive to the stimulus of present things as to be unconscious of his role in creating them; so that, even before being torn apart, he is a character who exists in fragments. A regret of the moralist of art is that the reward for the artist's unique sacrifice can never be timely enough. But this comes from mistaking admiration of Orpheus's music for direct sympathy with Orpheus. The truth is that his music, like the poet's words, is curiously indifferent to him, as for that matter it is to any wisdom it may seem to manifest:

But how late to be regretting all this, even
Bearing in mind that regrets are always late, too late!
To which Orpheus, a bluish cloud with white contours,
Replies that these are of course not regrets at all,
Merely a careful, scholarly setting down of
Unquestioned facts, a record of pebbles along the way.
And no matter how all this disappeared,
Or got where it was going, it is no longer
Material for a poem. Its subject
Matters too much, and not enough, standing there helplessly
While the poem streaked by, its tail afire, a bad
Comet screaming hate and disaster, but so turned inward
That the meaning, good or other, can never
Become known. The singer thinks
Constructively, builds up his chant in progressive stages
Like a skyscraper, but at the last minute turns away.
The song is engulfed in an instant in blackness
Which must in turn flood the whole continent
With blackness, for it cannot see. The singer
Must then pass out of sight, not even relieved
Of the evil burthen of the words. Stellification
Is for the few, and comes about much later
When all record of these people and their lives
Has disappeared into libraries, onto microfilm.
A few are still interested in them. "But what about
So-and-so?" is still asked on occasion. But they lie
Frozen and out of touch until an arbitrary chorus
Speaks of a totally different incident with a similar name
In whose tale are hidden syllables
Of what happened so long before that
In some small town, one indifferent summer.

In showing how the poet's words recede into a name, then a tale, and at last hidden syllables that tell of an unknown place, "Syringa" concludes with an observation on art in general. Wherever the center of attention appears to be, it will turn out that the action was somewhere else.

The long line and the calmly elaborating syntax of this poem are, in fact, borrowed from Auden's "Musée des Beaux Arts," which makes a similar point more explicitly. The result feels unexceptional in a poet whose sense of the decorum of style is faultless almost everywhere. Yet the very presence of the echo suggests a revision of Auden's teaching. His poem told us that we could isolate a note in the song or a figure in the painting even if the old masters never helped us by displaying it prominently. This was in keeping with Auden's belief that wisdom, even if only the wisdom of human limitation, could be derived from art for the sake of life. But Ashbery supposes that the observations of art enter our life as knowledge when it is already too late. About suffering, his old masters are never wrong because they are never right; and how could they be, when the suffering includes their own? As for the scholarly setting down of "unquestioned facts" about their careers, it is concerned with just the things they themselves do not regard. Meanwhile, their words have been withdrawn, leaving a blank that engulfs "the whole continent" in blackness. If the words return at all, it will be as "a totally different incident with a similar name." Ashbery's trope for the place of such recurrences is "some small town, one indifferent summer"; in "Self-Portrait in a Convex Mirror," he called it "pockets out of time." What he points to in either case is the inscrutability of change in art as in history. To put it another way, revision is the later reader's word for invention, and originality is his name for success that could be repeated under a new aspect. But for the poet, "not even relieved / Of the evil burthen of the words," both of these ideas are unintelligible.

The poet's ambition has been merely to become a totally different incident with a similar name, that is, to achieve ignorance of himself through his singing. To others eager for self-knowledge, this makes him "a bad / Comet screaming hate and disaster, but so turned inward / That the meaning, good or other, can never become known." It will not do to translate his ignorance as a side effect of conscious boldness. He is a disaster even to himself. And in these circumstances, the burden of the survival of his words is such that he would prefer to be relieved of it. "Stellification / Is for the few"—the we'll-make-you-a-star

syndrome being the invention of later readers and not of poets—
but how many would want it anyway? At the end of "Syringa"
one realizes how far perfection of the work, as Ashbery reads it,
must be from any appearance of conflict with perfection of the
life. The two have no relation to each other at all. The poet's
individual disasters or windfalls, if he has either in a notable
degree, will be taken as they are dealt out, free of any connection
with the energy that his words carry past him. Ashbery's
understanding of these matters has enabled him to appear in his
writing as at once the most confident and the least arrogant of
poets.

> —David Bromwich, "John Ashbery: The Self Against Its Images,"
> *Raritan* 5:4 (Spring 1986): 36–41.

JOHN SHOPTAW ON THE SONG LOST IN ITS SINGING

[In another extract from his book on Ashbery, Shoptaw
interprets the poem as an attempt to elegize the past
without getting stuck there.]

"Syringa" (written in 1975), one of Ashbery's finest poems, is in
many ways the most ambitious undertaking in *Houseboat Days*.
Like "Self-Portrait," "Syringa" begins with a given subject
matter, the myth of Orpheus and Eurydice, which may account
in part for the poem's popularity. Yet "Syringa," which maintains
the third person throughout, is not the elegy its underlying
narrative might lead us to expect. It lacks the sentimental pathos
of its humble companion-piece, "Street Musicians," for instance,
and the personal intensity of "Wet Casements." Eurydice
appears mainly as an afterthought. "Orpheus liked the glad
personal quality / Of the things beneath the sky," Ashbery
begins, adding quickly, "Of course, Eurydice was a part / Of this"
(HBD 69). Ashbery's Orpheus derives from Ovid's, who, after
losing Eurydice a second time, set an example to the Thracians
by loving boys (*Metamorphoses* X). This retelling of the Orpheus
myth will show us how to sing the past without looking back for
it.

The title "Syringa" sends us in several directions. Flowers of the genus syringa include the mock orange—a saxifrage like "the tiny, sparkling yellow flowers / Growing around the brink of the quarry" (HBD 70)—and the "lilac," Whitman's fragrant metonymy, preserving the consonants of "Lincoln," who remains unnamed in Whitman's elegy. But Ashbery, who dons the mantle of the historian rather than the mourner, espousing not cathartic but accurate songs, keeps his loss, if there was one, unrecoverable. "Syringa" also points toward Syrinx, an Arcadian nymph who was pursued by Pan, changed into a reed, and finally turned into a "syrinx" or "panpipe" by her frustrated lover (the story is told by Ovid in *Metamorphoses* I). But Pan passes unmentioned in "Syringa," and Syrinx is only fleetingly glimpsed in "the tossing reeds of that slow, / Powerful stream" (HBD 70). Moreover, the consolation prize of song, awarded to both Pan and Orpheus, is insufficient for Ashbery, who argues that "it isn't enough / To just go on singing" (HBD 70) as though nothing had happened. What might be called the elegiac myth of poetry, that the death or loss of the subject is the birth or gain of the song, offers this singer little comfort. He cannot hold on to his song, "Syringa," any more than to its vanished subject matter. Like Keats's "Ode to a Nightingale," the reflexive "Syringa" is its own elegy; it laments the song lost in its singing?[27]

"Syringa" begins like "Street Musicians," with an oval "O" and a sudden break—the egg of "Orpheus" dividing into three successive instances of the capitalized genitive "Of." Oneness shatters in the threadbare formula in which everything and nothing gets related: "Then one day, everything changed" (HBD 69). In response to the grief of Orpheus the sympathetic blue egg of the sky seems about to fall: "The sky shudders from one horizon / To the other, almost ready to give up wholeness" (HBD 69). Yeats's "shudder in the loins," which engendered history's tragic egg in "Leda and the Swan,"[28] certainly reverberates in Ashbery's sky. The crack in Nature is compounded by the rift between the present and the past, personified by a chiding Apollo: "'Leave it all on earth. / Your lute, what point? Why pick at a dull pavan few care to / Follow.... / Not vivid performances of the past'" (HBD 69).[29] Coming from the god of music, the question challenges; no historically minded poet can evade it. Harold Bloom claims, on the dust jacket of *Self-Portrait in a Convex Mirror*, that Ashbery "is joining that American sequence that includes Whitman, Dickinson, Stevens, and Hart Crane." Ashbery heeds his precursors, "tall guardians / Of yesterday," at the beginning of "Business Personals" (a poem he associates with "Syringa"[30]):

> The disquieting muses again: what are "leftovers"?
> Perhaps they have names for it all, who come bearing
> Worn signs of privilege whose authority
> Speaks out of the accumulation of age and faded colors
> To the center of today. Floating heart, why
> Wander on senselessly? The tall guardians
> Of yesterday are steep as cliff shadows;
> Whatever path you take abounds in their sense.
> (HBD 18)

Though Ashbery has his own ideas about influence, one could not ask for a more trenchant restatement of Bloom's theory. Before Orpheus can reply to Apollo's Bloomian challenge, the narrator cuts in and answers for him: "But why not? / All other things must change too." "The seasons," like the poets, "are no longer what they once were," but their faded virtues fit each other (HBD 69). Only contemporaries, the argument goes, speak to contemporary reality.

"Syringa" argues for "change," the English word for Ovid's "metamorphosis." Ashbery speaks against the kind of ahistorical "epistemological snapshot" that stereotyped him in "Wet Casements": "For although memories, of a season, for example, / Melt into a single snapshot, one cannot guard, treasure / That stalled moment. It too is flowing, fleeting" (HBD 70). Though this passage, which now seems to augur *Flow Chart*, puts everything into flux, we shouldn't conclude, for instance, that Ashbery doesn't have "treasured memories" or that his poetry precludes climactic, epiphanic moments. Like Proust and Wordsworth before him, Ashbery has learned that one must turn away from the frontal happiness of those prophetic moments in order to keep them. In the epiphany of "Syringa," one of the towering moments in Ashbery's poetry, the portentous poem itself flashes away:

                         Its subject
Matters too much, and not enough, standing there helplessly
While the poem streaked by, its tail afire, a bad
Comet screaming hate and disaster, but so turned inward
That the meaning, good or other, can never
Become known. The singer thinks
Constructively, builds up his chant in progressive stages
Like a skyscraper, but at the last minute turns away.
The song is engulfed in an instant in blackness
Which must in turn flood the whole continent
With blackness, for it cannot see.
(HBD 71)

The turn away avoids Orpheus's error of regarding but still loses
"The song" to "blackness." Such eclipses dot Ashbery's career,
from "The Mythological Poet" to "Clepsydra" to the end of
"The New Spirit," and on to the "cimmerian moment" of "A
Wave." The blind prophetic moment engulfs the poet's Tower in
"flames" (under "blackness"). But what kind of blind, charred
construction remains? For a poem to change, the poet must
relinquish its Eurydicean "subject / Matters." As the singer
"turns away," his construction is "turned inward." Ashbery's
poetics are in this regard essentially new-critical: "I think of my
poems as independent objects or little worlds which are self-
referential."[31] But this introversion is above all defensively self-
reflexive, protecting its final meaning from critics who would
judge it prematurely. Citing Shakespeare's Hector, Ashbery
remarks that "The end crowns all" so long as the towers of Troy
are still standing (HBD 70; *Troilus and Cressida*, IV, v, 224). As in
"Street Musicians," introversion also lets the poet keep the past
by unknowingly imitating it. "Syringa" ends with the singers
buried in the library stacks,

Frozen and out of touch until an arbitrary chorus
Speaks of a totally different incident with a similar name
In whose tale are hidden syllables
Of what happened so long before that
In some small town, one indifferent summer.
(HBD 71)

The rebirth Ashbery describes here resembles his own unintentional procedure of composing by crypt words. We don't know—nor perhaps does Ashbery—what syllables are hidden here, or whether this concluding "summer," recalling the end of "Daffy Duck" and Roussel's "The View," is confessional or representative. But few of us would imagine that such a summer was "indifferent."

What makes the summer, and the elegiac poet, "indifferent"? As in "Scheherazade," the adjective completes the typical range of judgments, "good, bad, or indifferent," launched by the "bad / Comet" ("comment") and the "meaning, good or other." The poet's meteoric rise should pass without comment or judgment, even from its author. Earlier still, we were warned that music, like time and Eurydice, "passes, emblematic / Of life and how you cannot isolate a note of it / And say it is good or bad" (HBD 70). When we and the past no longer matter to each other, like a pair of indifferent lovers, we can sing accurately. So too the good poet remains indifferent to bad comets. In a Stevensian mood, Ashbery asserts that "Singing accurately"—in a nonce word (merging "encapsulates" and "epitomizes")—"encapsulizes /The different weights of the things" (HBD 70). In his elegy for his teacher Santayana, Stevens, singer of "accurate songs" (214), instructs himself to "Be orator but with an accurate tongue / And without eloquence" (372). Ashbery's Orpheus makes a similar, self-reflexive claim for veracity: "these are of course not regrets at all, / Merely a careful, scholarly setting down of / Unquestioned facts, a record of pebbles along the way" (HBD 71; "peoples"). Does critical detachment translate into aesthetic distance? The author, "standing there helplessly / While the poem" is judged good, bad, or indifferent, must remain indifferent to his own canonization or oblivion. Ashbery realizes that "Stellification / Is for the few, and comes about much later" (HBD 71).

NOTES

27. The best discussion of this elegiac myth of poetry is found in Peter M. Sacks, *The English Elegy: Studies in the Genre from Spenser to Yeats* (Baltimore: Johns Hopkins UP, 1985) 1–37. For a fascinating discussion of Elliott Carter's setting of "Syringa," see Lawrence Kramer, *Music and Poetry: The Nineteenth Century and After* (Berkeley: California, 1984) 203–21.

28. William Butler Yeats, *The Collected Poems of W. B. Yeats*, ed. Richard J. Finneran (New York: Macmillan, 1989) 214. All citations of Yeats's poetry are from this edition, cited hereafter in the text.

29. This challenge from Apollo originates in Callimachus (*Aetia*, I), a famous passage adapted by Virgil in his sixth eclogue.

30. Ashbery explained the title in a 1976 reading: "in some newspapers before the personals and after the classified ads there is a sort of gray area of business personals, which are really not very personal, people who have guitars for sale and things like that. I was wondering about the way in which they were personal, which caused me to begin writing this poem. The first line is a reference not to Sylvia Plath but to a painting by de Chirico." Rec. 16 May 1976, Lamont Library, Harvard University.

31. Labrie 31.

—John Shoptaw, *On the Outside Looking Out* (Cambridge: Harvard Univ. Press, 1994): 209–212.

"A Wave"

Forced by an interviewer to concede a central motif in his work, Ashbery once said "As I have gotten older, it seems to me that time is what I have been writing about all these years during which I thought I wasn't writing about anything." Perhaps more than any of his other poems, "A Wave" addresses each of these interconnected admissions: a) I am getting older and need to face this fact, b) I do have a subject matter, although c) I and many others are often convinced that I have none.

At the time he wrote "A Wave," Ashbery was nearly sixty and had been advocating, to borrow Marjorie Perloff's phrase, a "poetics of indeterminacy" for almost forty years. That is a long time to be skating on the thin ice of an "invisible terrain." Much to Ashbery's surprise, however, a whole host of other poets, professors, and prize committees had ploughed their way through intimidating banks of white noise to join him out on that frozen lake. In many of his later works, one gets the sense that an older, heavier Ashbery, feeling responsible for this precarious assembly, has dropped to his knees and is peering down through the ice to see just how thick it really is and whether anything of note hides in the black water beneath. Among other things, "A Wave" is an extended record of those soundings.

What he finds is no mere lake but "an ocean of language" and rather than shoring oneself against it, he advises inundation. "A Wave" thus begins with three small cracks in the retaining wall between the structures of traditional poetics and the rough yet exhilarating seas of the poem. Each of the opening sentences is fragmentary, seemingly lifted at random from different minds, different poems. They serve as mental palate cleansers, wiping the canvas clean and transporting the reader onto the "invisible terrain" that Ashbery is about to explore. But, like the opening lines of "Self-Portrait," they also contain metonymic references to Ashbery's larger aesthetic concerns: "to pass through pain" is what we all must do during the course of our lives, "and not know it" an ambiguous addendum that suggests both the possibility of discovering, through poetry, a new way of understanding that painful passage of time and an implicit admission of the confusion experienced in the interim; "a car door slamming in the night" evokes a sudden conscious moment, the kind of shocked awakening to the ever-present now that Ashbery has been writing about in one way or another since the beginning; and "to emerge on an invisible terrain" is the anticipated aftermath of that awakening, the "ambition" retained from "Soonest Mended" to "step free at last, minuscule on the gigantic plateau." But, as we saw with that earlier reexamination, the "gigantic plateau" may in fact be a mirage, not so much a destination as a Moebius strip of infinite return.

The second stanza recedes, makes a little more sense, but still lacks the *terra firma* of a context. It is "partially out of focus." The words pantomime meaning like a "mute actor." Both Ashbery and the reader now inhabit a "middle distance" where "people and plants" call "attention to themselves with every artifice of which the human / Genre is capable." This middle distance is both invitation and disclaimer, "a haven of serenity and unreachable," its "artifice" the source of its greatest appeal and its ultimate weakness.

By the third stanza we have fully embarked for Ashbery territory, a place forever on "the threshold / Of love and desperation," where nameless things sing elegies "At night...in the black trees" for something missing and "mindless." Just as soon as we determine the day of the week and the mood of the weather, "all of sudden the scene changes" to "another idea, a new conception." Before long the reader "emerges on the other side," already beginning to understand this state of "tragic euphoria" is not some temporary derangement of the senses but life itself, the vibrant greenhouse "in which your spirit sprouted. And which is justified in you."

And on it goes, for twenty-one more pages—"the tale will stretch on / For miles before it is done." Currents of thought come and go like jet streams, carrying with them their own chaotic weather systems and schools of life. On one hand, the only way to properly enjoy the voyage is to let go of the rudder, for only when "the issue / Of making sense becomes such a far-off one" can the "mesmerizing plan of the landscape [become] / At last apparent." On the other hand, there's always a chance that nothing will be "revealed" but "more detritus." Although the potential for a novel destination or new understanding seems to exist—"Still it is better this way / Than to have to live through a sequence of events acknowledged / In advance in order to get to a primitive statement"—the validity of this underlying assumption will be constantly questioned throughout the rest of the poem.

In fact, the eschaton or ultimate destiny towards which "A Wave" builds is one of anti-epiphany and "strangeness," leavened only by intermittent moments of lucidity and love. About midway through the poem, the reader is nearly drowned by a textual tsunami in the form of a twenty-seven line sentence (beginning mid-line with "That can't concern us" and ending with "encountered eternity in the meantime") that is followed, shortly thereafter, by a "cimmerian moment in which all lives, all destinies / And incompleted destinies were swamped / As though by a giant wave that picks itself up / Out of a calm sea and retreats again into nowhere." Here Ashbery again turns to classical allusion for emphasis and added weight. The Cimmerians were a mythical people described by Homer as dwelling in a remote realm of mist and gloom. Instead of the "infrequent pellucid moments" that define life for most poets, Ashbery focuses on the "strangeness" of the "empty page" upon which those moments are "inscribed," and envisions an apocalyptic "cimmerian moment" that wipes the slate clean entirely. If this sounds too much like nihilism, one should remember that the original nihilists were revolutionaries, not lazy-minded naysayers. In any case, Ashbery has already self-inflicted any damage you can do to his underlying philosophy (provided you can even pin one down). Towards the end of "A Wave" he suggests that "perhaps it's too late for anything like the overhaul / That seemed called for, earlier." Moreover, though Ashbery leaves his readers adrift at the poem's conclusion ("But all was strange."), his poetry, his "knotted rope of guesswork" provides, in and of itself, a lifeline of sorts, strengthened by his winking promise that "we'll / Stay in touch."

CRITICAL VIEWS ON

"A Wave"

JAMES APPLEWHITE ON ASHBERY AND ABSTRACTION

[James Applewhite is a Professor of Creative Writing and
American Literature at Duke University. He is the author
of seven books of poetry as well as numerous works of
literary criticism, including *Seas and Inland Journeys:
Landscape and Consciousness from Wordsworth to Roethke.* In
this extract, Applewhite explains the intent and effect of
Ashbery's non-referential style.]

As with abstract expressionist paintings, the issue of reference in
Ashbery's poems is difficult. Of course it is not true to say that
Ashbery has no subject matter. His subject is the process of the
psyche, its verbal reactions, during its being in the world. But is
that so broad a subject as to be no subject in particular? Does the
disjunction between this verbal consciousness and its social and
natural environment rule out any recognizable correspondence
between the subjective and the objective? The world *does* enter
into Ashbery's meditations, but it is by bits and pieces. All the
things, individually, are recognizable, but we miss the identifiable
sequences, the movements and actions and purposes ordered as
society expects them to be ordered.

In the title poem of *A Wave* there is a point at which this
disjunction seems to be recognized and even partially explained.

> But in the end the dark stuff, the odd quick attack
> Followed by periods of silence that get shorter and shorter
> Resolves the subjective-versus-objective approach by undoing
> The complications of our planet, its climate, its sonatinas
> And stories, its patches of hard ugly snow waiting around
> For spring to melt them.

Though "the dark stuff" (especially if in apposition with "odd
quick attack") remains abundantly mysterious, we can recognize
that this resolution-by-undoing follows a sense of loss or of

psychic breaching. After the comparison of two opposed landscape-structures suggestive of the process of growing up to face oneself and the world, there is

> the breached sense of your own being
> To live with, to somehow nurse back to plenitude:
> Yet it never again has that hidden abundance.

Part, at least, of what the poet recalls having fallen out of tune with is the expected correspondence between the psyche's conformation and society's structures of expectation: those tableaus we call *meaning*. In the first, more realistic sequence of development, the poet encounters the world as it is, the walkways looking dangerous, but is able to "stand up more clearly / To the definition" of what he is. This freedom involves a dismantling, a state "when all attributes / Are sinking in the maelstrom of de-definition." The opposite possibility is presented in a beautiful, nostalgic "picture," a dreamlike illusion of coming "home" to some quintessentially American place/time.

> I was lost, but seemed to be coming home,
> Through quincunxes of apple trees, but ever
> As I drew closer, as in Zeno's paradox, the mirage
> Of home withdrew and regrouped a little farther off.
> I could see white curtains fluttering at the windows
> And in the garden under a big brass-tinted apple tree
> The old man had removed his hat and was gazing at the grass
> As though in sorrow, sorrow for what I had done.

The aura of Adamic fall (in apple tree and Jehovah-figure sorrowing over son's disobedience) survives the abstraction. Here the fall takes the shape of a failure of relation between the sanctioned, recognizable *home* and the beholding psyche:

> Realizing it was now or never, I lurched
> With one supreme last effort out of the dream
> Onto the couch-grass behind the little red-painted palings:
> I was here! But it all seemed so lonesome. I was welcomed
> Without enthusiasm. My room had been kept as it was
> But the windows were closed, there was a smell of a closed room.

The speaker's inability to relate to this idyll, this sanctioned, recognizable, "representational" landscape, is thus a loss and a freedom. It results in an undoing of the world's ordinary complications, its sonatinas and melting snow, and a substitution of unique, abstract landscapes of the poet's own devising. There is the *sense*, the atmosphere, of the external, its iron bulk and pressure. There is the enemy's "message like iron trenches under ground / That rise here and there in blunt, undulating shapes." But there are no ordinary events, only the interpretations, the way things feel, their ominousness and oddity. The last sentence of the book: "But all was strange." We have thus tone without situation, climate without particular landscape, expression without the song. We have the style of the world and the style of the mind, and the style of their relation and nonrelation. Signs removed from their usual sequences (marriages, journeys) are situated within a medium of sensibility whose style we call Ashbery.

—James Applewhite, "Painting, Poetry, Abstraction, and Ashbery," *The Southern Review* 24:2 (Spring 1988): 283–285.

KEVIN CLARK ON THE STRUCTURE BENEATH THE SURFACE

[Kevin Clark is a Professor of English at California Polytechnic State University and an award-winning poet. In addition to three chapbooks and one full-length collection of verse, he has written numerous articles on contemporary poetry. In this extract from an article on the poem, Clark unearths a more conventional, Symbolist technique underpinning the indeterminacy for which Ashbery is more commonly known.]

That Ashbery believes long poems are "much closer to a whole reality" than shorter poems is telling. Despite their sometimes inhibiting length and poetics, his own long poems written since 1975 are considerably closer not only to "a whole reality" but to conventional poetic technique, one which few critics acknowledge. One of his most brilliant critics is Marjorie Perloff, who without making a distinction between long and short poems, maintains that Ashbery's poetry is distinguished by an enigmatic style which privileges indeterminacy rather than the traditional symbolist style practiced by most modernist and postmodernist poets. I would like here to refine Perloff's thesis by suggesting that, while Ashbery makes much use of this enigmatic style in his long poems, passages characterized by such a style are blended into and subordinated to a dominant symbolist technique, rendering his later long poems surprisingly conventional and more easily interpretable. A good example is his most recent long poem, "A Wave" (1984).[1]

Taken from the book by the same title, "A Wave" is characterized by the poet's desire to represent experience as ongoing impression, "the tender blur of the setting" (69). Where most poets write as if meaning can be gathered from distinctly unique or intense episodes, Ashbery—particularly in his more recent long poems—insists that only a sense of meaning can be felt, and this only for short periods.

> And the issue of making sense becomes such a far-off one.
> Isn't this "sense"—
> This little dog of my life that I can see—that answers me
> Like a dog, and wags its tails, though excitement and fidelity are
> About all that ever gets expressed? (70)

While his subject here may be the indeterminacy of consciousness, his writing is conventionally referential. By "sense" of meaning he intends the emotional world we inhabit. Since the publication of "Self-Portrait in a Convex Mirror" (1975), Ashbery's long poems render this interior world so accurately by transmitting such a multitude of deceptively casual musings, like the one above, that the ideas give way to effect: we retain the impression of a human being continually engaging elementary questions about life more than we retain any of the specific questions or answers. Meaning is not forgotten, but, because Ashbery seems always to doubt but never entirely reject the *possibility* of meaning, we are left with a notion of his continuing uncertainty.

But this is not to say his long poems are afloat, unfixed in a universe of non sequiturs. Most of Ashbery's recent long poems are accessible, though their style can seem at first prohibitively resistant to understanding. Eventually, competent readers can find that the truly enigmatic passages are blended with those of reasonably straightforward language to produce an impression of the conscious mind in alternating periods of perplexity and clarity. And throughout the poem, Ashbery nearly announces his technique as well as his point of view. He is not evasive; he is referential—that is to say, he employs symbolist tools.

Perloff sees symbolist writing as that kind described by Eliot in his call for an objective correlative. In Eliot's words, the "only way of expressing emotion in the form of art is by finding 'an objective correlative'; in other words, a set of objects, a situation, a chain of events which shall be the formula of that particular emotion ..." (145). Perloff also turns to Auden's claim that a poet may describe the "sacred encounters of his imagination" in terms of something other than the components of that encounter (58). Surely Perloff is correct in her translation of Eliot's and Auden's poetics, contending that the two High Modernists were committed to a style of writing which renders even the "ineffable" through "concretion of the symbol" (27). Her notion of symbolist writing is nothing new: words signifying discernible referents outside the poem. But focusing on the poet's early verse, Perloff asserts that an Ashbery poem, regardless of length, cuts off "the referential dimension" (266) and that his images usually "have no discernible referents" (267).

For the sake of discussion, then, let us think of the term "symbolist" as nearly synonymous with "referential." Symbolist poetry usually achieves meaning by means of a system of imagery which renders an idea or attitude. In this sense, most poems are symbolist. Those that are not are poems which intentionally sabotage their own grammar in order to call into question conventional poetic processes for communicating. Rimbaud, Stein, Olsen, and even Pound, in certain cantos, practiced variations of such an antisymbolist poetics. Today, while language poets are most actively antisymbolist, their poems are rarely long. (Michael Palmer's "Notes for Echo Lake" [1981] is an exception). (...)

In "A Wave" there exists for the narrator the assumption that there had been an earlier stage in life which was continually fulfilling, when metaphysical anxieties were unnecessary and the spirit was happily replete. But that time of unexamined childlike confidence was abandoned for an adult self-assessment made difficult by a nearly ceaseless skepticism and an equally skeptical approach to that skepticism. The result is the present tentative self-consciousness he describes, a perpetual state of trustlessness. Accordingly, "A Wave" has two subjects: how to comprehend experience when it seems so ephemeral and how to experience love when it, too, is necessarily evanescent, being only a part of the larger experiential realm.

While "A Wave" begins with several difficult passages, the poem grows increasingly philosophical and accessible, though not committing itself to the subject of love until about a quarter of the way through. Here, Ashbery doesn't so much announce his subject, but rather describes it in passing. First, he is discussing a sense of new purpose:

> And no special sense of decline ensued
> But perhaps a few moments of music of such tact
> and weariness
> That one awakens with a new sense of purpose.... (72)

But, still concerned with this "new sense of purpose," he mentions:

> I am prepared to deal with this
> While putting together notes related to the question of love
> For the many, for two people at once, and for myself
> In a time of need unlike those that have arisen so far. (73)

Thus the poem's intention is declared: the poet will simultaneously discuss twin positives in his life—purpose and love. But of both we can only have some vague understanding. For Ashbery, life occurs, and only rarely are we sensitive to the details of our passing through it, each of us alone in our usual dim state:

      stand with you as you mope and thrash
            your way through time,
      Imagining it as it is, a kind of tragic euphoria
      In which your spirit sprouted. (68–69)

Because we necessarily must live our lives in the dishevelment of
shifting feelings rather than the clarity of confident knowing, we
receive life as impression. Each moment continually gives way to the
next, being assimilated into a vague supposition based on the past.
We cannot constantly compute our positions, and thus Ashbery
frequently resorts to the most important word in the poem's lexicon:
sense. We retain a *sense* of life and of ourselves, and very little more.

Sometimes that sense is, indeed, very vague. During such
moments, we gain what Ashbery sees as a "sense" of confusion,
which he sometimes illustrates with amusing blocks of
bewildering logical connections, very much like the shorter
poems. These passages seem to be communicating something
about the inevitability of quotidian events. Meaning appears to
be real, only hidden or just around the corner.

But again Ashbery does not engage in so indeterminate a style
for long, and, just as the quotidian can begin to make some sense
at times, his verse becomes increasingly clearer. This is not to say
that he believes in belief, so to speak, but that his language
resorts once more to dealing with incertitude in a
comprehensible manner. Inevitably he shifts back to a more
understandable poetic language in order to describe the
relationship between attempts at categorizing experience and
what that experience will actually come to be. Meaning thus lies
not in the "crispness" of rational understanding, but in "a density
of ... opinion" (AW 69–70) which, because it is not and cannot be
carefully calculated, must be a feeling, a "sense" formed of
suspended conjecture. The poem consists of a continuing series
of Kafkaesque reactions and counterreactions.

      We had, though, a feeling of security
      But we weren't aware of it then: that's
      How secure we were. (75)

Ashbery often uses the words "so" and "and" to propel the poem along against the impediments thrown up by "yet" and "but." Back and forth, the potential contests against the disempowering.

Unlike Stevens, Ashbery is rarely conclusively satisfied; unwilling to forego his "questioning side," he suggests a state of existence in which the processes of the poem continue after the poem's finish until our own demise:

> And so each of us has to remain alone, conscious of
> > each other
> Until the day when war absolves us of our differences. We'll
> Stay in touch. *So* they have it, all the time. But all was
> > strange. (89)

Here Ashbery is not only unwilling to forego his circular doubt, but he is also unwilling to finish the poem on purely symbolist terms. "They" is a sudden, inexplicable intrusion, suggesting perhaps "our differences," or former lovers, or more probably the existence of greater random forces which we cannot control.

The quotations above demonstrate that "A Wave" is not a radically fragmented, enigmatic, inaccessible piece of writing. Certainly, many of Ashbery's signature devices appear throughout the poem: the unclear pronoun references, the long sentence fragments, the cleverly misplaced modifiers, the intentional reliance on amorphous, beguiling generalizations. At times, he reverses the process of Eliotic fragmentation by using conventionally logical connectives to link illogically related notions; at other times, he splices nonsensical ideas together by linking them to a single common event. Yet only the opening of the poem is as particularly puzzling as the shorter, purely enigmatic poems. The grammar becomes more conventional and the poem becomes progressively comprehensible as it probes its themes.

Sometime before the publication of "Self-Portrait," Ashbery said that he had been "attempting to keep meaningfulness up to the pace of randomness ... I really think meaningfulness can't get along without randomness and that they somehow have to be brought together" (*Craft* 121).[3] "A Wave" is certainly an attempt to do just that: to grant the poem a symbolist logic while also rendering the sudden moments of confusion and incertitude we often encounter in the course of a day, let alone the course of a lifetime. Generally his writing is symbolist when he *tells* us and enigmatic when he *shows* us. The lasting effect of this blend is to endow the reader with an impression of a consciousness energized by a desire to question while enervated by a propensity to doubt.

NOTES

1. "A Wave" is approximately 700 lines in length, stretched over 29 irregular stanzas. Because Ashbery's long poem "As We Know" is actually two poems in one, designed to be read simultaneously, it is to some extent different from "A Wave" or "Self-Portrait in a Convex Mirror," and for that reason it is beyond the scope of this paper. However, most of this discussion could be applied to "As We Know."

3. I first realized the importance of this quote when reading Kalstone 187.

WORKS CITED

Ashbery, John. *The Craft of Poetry: Interviews from the New York Quarterly*. New York: Doubleday, 1974.

———. *Self-Portrait in a Convex Mirror*. New York: Viking, 1975.

———. *A Wave*. New York: Viking, 1984.

Auden, W. H. "Making, Knowing, and judging." *The Dyer's Hand and Other Essays*. 1962. New York: Vintage, 1968.

Eliot, T. S. "Hamlet." *Selected Essays*. London: Faber, 1953.

Kalstone, David. *Five Temperaments*. Oxford: Oxford UP, 1977.

Perloff, Marjorie. *The Poetics of Indeterminacy*. Princeton: Princeton UP, 1981.

—Kevin Clark, "John Ashbery's 'A Wave': Privileging the Symbol," *Papers on Language and Literature* 26:2 (Spring 1990): 271–279.

EDWARD HAWORTH HOEPPNER ON THE LIMITS OF NOW

[Edward Haworth Hoeppner is a Professor of English at Oakland University. A widely published poet, Hoeppner has also written a study of Ashbery and W. S. Merwin, from which the following is drawn. In this extract, he argues that the poem reveals in Ashbery a new acceptance of the influence of the past and future on the present.]

"A Wave" accepts what Ashbery's poems have so often been refused: the notion that the past is influential, that it stands apart from and qualifies our attention to the present rather than streams from the moment as the residue of activity or imagination. Not that the past can be reembodied, but it can restore to the present "a new, separate life." That new life depends on the future, however, on the apocalyptic end of language when names are completely "removed from things," and so the self is caught in what it can restore and in the landscape of the present that it must "go on despising until that day when environment / Finally reads as a necessary but still vindictive opposition" to "all caring, all explaining" (*W*, 77–78). Thus it is restoration that the poem finally questions, in part because "separate life" becomes a sentence to confinement in time rather than a novel innocence.

Dayan's contention that "A Wave" is both a "program for purification" and a "deliberate effort to know," that it is a meditation on love in which "knowing" becomes "part and parcel of the desiring body," hints at its major difficulty.[51] "Caring" and "explaining" so configure the other that it stands always beyond Ashbery's immediacy. He is left with a desire that his language, stuck to the life of the self and "battening" on the present, can hardly address. Like the "deliberate attempt" to practice "ease of address" and "immediacy" that Merwin makes in "St. Vincent's," Ashbery's meditations in "A Wave" deliberate the self by exposing practice to its nemesis. The "all," as indifference, is not available to the "separate" self that cares and wants to explain, and persistence in "knowing" love casts the future into the present in terms of ultimate loss. The "possibility of something more liberated and gracious" is only available beyond language and life. It is "dust at the pores" of *would*, a possibility "not of this time."

Having held forth so long against closure, in which the body of language replicates transcendence and limit in the metaphors of climax and denouement, Ashbery has made cerebration, attention to life, the pulse of time. But if he has this way augmented duration in individual poems, the climactic past and the large denouement, death, loom increasingly large in "A

Wave." In one sense it is time so framed that represents freedom, if it will be so "gracious" as to put an end to language. The past presages its final stroke in this poem, and time figures as a vertical check on any attempt to restore to the self an infinite duration. It becomes a counterweight to absorption in perception:

> So the voluminous past
> Accepts, recycles our claims to present consideration
> And the urban landscape is once again untroubled, smooth
> As wax. As soon as the oddity is flushed out
> It becomes monumental and anxious once again, looking
> Down on our lives as from a baroque pinnacle and not the
> Mosquito that was here twenty minutes ago.
> The past absconds
> With our fortunes just as we were rounding a major
> Bend in the swollen river; not to see ahead
> Becomes the only predicament when what
> Might be sunken there is mentioned only
> In crabbed allusions but will be back tomorrow.
>
> (*W*, 78)

In the "monumental" past "looking down" on the present Ashbery also invokes the future, so that "our fortunes," what is not seen, is foreshadowed as loss. Because he couples the landscape of today to finality, the subjects of "A Wave"—the devastations of love and time—produce some rather uncharacteristic expressions: "the empty space in the endless continuum / of time has come up: the space that can be filled only by you" (*W*, 79); and "being alone at the center of a moan that did not issue from me / And is pulling me back toward old forms of address" (*W*, 80). But the poem's chief accomplishment is to make the moment of desire punctuate the self so that duration becomes the victim as well as the vanguard of time. "The cimmerian moment in which all lives" is "swamped / As though by a giant wave" (*W*, 81). The surface does not suffice, and the present does not "restore" the self.

There are three options for love in "A Wave." It may be an absence not yet felt, "the seemingly blessed may be unaware of having lost it"; it may be never realized, as for "the luckless" who "describe love in glowing terms to strangers / In taverns"; and it may be desire constantly approached, satisfied, and redirected, as it is for "a small remnant / Whose lives are congruent with their souls / And who ever afterward know no mystery in it" (*W*, 81). Rejecting love past or projected, the speaker identifies with the faithful whose souls refute mystery as ignorance or illusion (not with the "seemingly blessed" who are "unaware" of the way love fails, or with the "luckless" who buttonhole "strangers"). This decision locates satisfaction by binding love to recurrent desire, making it "congruent" to living. What "knowing" discovers, however, is that desiring is bound to loss, the reversals of fortune, the "giant wave" that absconds with the future:

> so it is the only way
> That love determines us, and we look the same
> To others when they happen in afterwards, and cannot even know
> We have changed, so massive in our difference
> We are, like a new day that looks and cannot be the same
> As those we used to reckon with, and so start
> On our inane rounds again too dumb to profit from past
> Mistakes—that's how different we are!
>
> (*W*, 81)

Here sameness so overcomes change that the present (routed as it is in a cyclical economy of repetition and loss) encodes the past and future. The fact that "others" do not "know" similarly restricts the self, and Ashbery's horror of stepping out of time becomes clear.

If, like love, the present in "A Wave" is framed by loss, it nonetheless avoids finality by temporizing desire, reconstituting the other in relative rather than absolute terms, and anticipating both the failure and renewal of that project. As long as time progresses without accumulating, the self can survive by recasting rather than enlarging upon its desire for the other:

> there is something else—call it a constant eventfulness,
> A common appreciation of the way things have of enfolding
> When your attention is distracted for a moment, and then

It's all bumps and history, as though this crusted surface
Had always been around, didn't just happen to come into being
A short time ago. The scarred afternoon is unfortunate
Perhaps, but as they come to see each other dimly
And for the first time, an internal romance
Of the situation rises in these human beings like sap
And they can at last know the fun of not having it all but
Having instead a keen appreciation of the ways in which it
Underachieves as well as rages: an appetite,
For want of a better word. In darkness and silence.

(W, 83)

"A Wave" passes through pain and *does* know it, however, and
Ashbery's fascination with the whole of things suffers diminution
in this "scarred afternoon": "the fun of not having it all" exposes
the shortcomings of love, and desire is reduced to an appetite that
rages and underachieves on the way to "darkness and silence."

Holding forth and prohibiting satisfaction, time is like Zeno's
paradox: the past recedes as it is incorporated. "Days each with
its disarming set of images and attitudes / Are beneficial
perhaps," but "only after the last one / In every series has
disappeared" (*W*, 87). So the future poses as always. In this light
the quotidian is an insecure constant.

Always, a few errands

Summon us periodically from the room of our forethought
And that is a good thing. And such attentiveness
Besides! Almost more than anybody could bring to anything.
But we managed it, and with good grace, too. Nobody
Is going to hold that against us. But since you bring up
    the question
I will say I am not unhappy to place myself entirely
At your disposal temporarily. Much that had been drained
    out of living
Returns, in those moments, mounting the little capillaries
Of polite questions and seeming concern. I want it back.

And although that other question that I asked and can't
Remember any more is going to move still further upward,
    casting

Its shadow enormously over where I remain, I can't see it.
Enough to know that I shall have answered for myself soon,
Be led away for further questioning and later returned
To the amazingly quiet room in which all my life has been spent.

(W, 89)

"Not unhappy," "temporarily," "I want it back"—these qualify
Ashbery's hope in an eschaton that will not reveal but dissolve
the word. Meanwhile the stoppage of time, a vertical stake set
somewhere in the future, throws a shadow on now. The
speaker is left with "the limited set of reflections we were given
at the beginning / To try to make a fortune out of," at least
until the time when his "radical stance" will "have had some
meaning,"

<blockquote>
and for itself, not for us who lie gasping
On slopes never having had the nerve to trust just us, to go
    out with us
Not fearing some solemn overseer in the breath from the
    treetops.
</blockquote>

(W, 88)

There is a bravery in this waiting, but it is finally Ashbery's
"amazingly quiet room," the "window that dominates
everything" a "little too much" (W, 88), which indicates how
trapped within perception the subject has become, an isolation
rendered all the more telling when being "led away" and "later
returned" to the moment of attention give way to death's
execution. Hence the dream of being absolved of "our
differences," and the flat promise to "stay in touch" with which
the poem closes. For being "in touch" falters when language
winds down for Ashbery, and touching, as a figure for identity,
falls prey to time.

NOTES

51. Dayan, "Finding What Will Suffice," 1067–69.

—Edward Haworth Hoeppner, *Echoes and Moving Fields: Structure
and Subjectivity in the Poetry of W. S. Merwin and John Ashbery*
(Lewisburg: Bucknell University press, 1994): 209–213.

DAVID HERD ON THE URGENCIES OF LOVE AND EXCLUSION

[In another extract from his book on Ashbery, Herd interprets "A Wave" as a crisis of homosexual identity.]

The problem for the critic of this magnificent long poem is that precisely because it calls such 'unimaginable diplomacy into being', it is exceedingly difficult to talk about.[29] So to be clear, the suggestion here is not that 'A Wave' is a poem about AIDS. To define it as such would be altogether to overlook the breathtakingly supple handling of the question of definition which is central to its purpose.[30] The suggestion rather is that if one were to try to imagine a poem which really took seriously the deeply intractable questions of definition implicit in the problems of community and identity that Jones and Edelman argue surface as a result of the AIDS crisis, then one might imagine a poem so appropriate to the situation as to be difficult to recognise as such. A poem so 'right', as Ashbery and Schuyler put it in *A Nest of Ninnies*, 'one cannot see it until its time is past' (NN, 181). Arguably 'A Wave' is such a poem. In a significant sense it is the consummate Ashbery long poem, providing the poetic summation the history of whose making is told by the shorter poems in the collection. As such it is deeply concerned with questions of community and identity. These concerns, and the relation between them, are faintly audible behind the title itself: a wave both threatening inundation and defying definition.

The poem opens with an image of suffering:

> To pass through pain and not know it,
> A car door slamming in the night.
> To emerge on an invisible terrain.   (W, 68)

What largely consumes 'A Wave', however, is not the extreme circumstance of pain, but the business of ordinary life; its extended sentences wrapped up in the events, memories, meetings, reflections, thoughts, speculations and desires which make up a life. We have encountered all this before in Ashbery, watched his writing 'mope and thrash [its] way though time' this way. There is a renewed vividness to the writing, 'the thing / Is there in all its interested variegatedness'. But this is, as the poem puts it, 'business as usual'. We have read it, or something like it, before in Ashbery.

Gradually, however, as history happens, and while the living is getting done, audibly urgent concerns begin to impinge on the poet's thinking. Some five pages into the poem an issue emerges which partially distracts him from the business of living. 'I am prepared', the poet tells us,

> to deal with this
> While putting together notes related to the question of love
> For the many, for two people at once, and for myself
> In a time of need unlike those that have arisen so far.
>
> (W, 73)

Love is one of the urgencies in the poem. Exclusion is another:

> No, the
> Divine tolerance we seem to feel is actually in short supply,
> And those moving forward toward us from the other end of the
> bridge
> Are defending, not welcoming us to, the place of power,
> A hill ringed with low, ridgelike fortifications.
>
> (W, 74)

A sense of helplessness in the midst of fear—of 'Being alone at the center of a moan that did not issue from me'—is another. These are aspects of a crisis, which, as it develops, comes increasingly to preoccupy the poem, until it can no longer absorb itself in the business of living, but must concern itself instead with both the

> business of living and dying, the orderly
> Ceremonials and handling of estates,
> Checking what does not appear normal and drawing together
> All the rest into the report that will finally be made
>
> (W, 80)

The gathering sense of crisis—marked here by the funereal language—culminates in two passages around which the energy and imagery of the poem appear to coalesce. The first has to do with a community in crisis, in that it contemplates

> The cimmerian moment in which all lives, all destinies
> And incompleted destinies were swamped
> As though by a giant wave that picks itself up
> Out of a calm sea and retreats again into nowhere
> Once its damage is done.
>
> (W, 81)

According to Greek mythology the Cimmerians were a people who lived in darkness at the edge of the world. They are, accordingly, the archetype of the marginal community. Except that here, in their moment of crisis, they appear less marginal than ever, the giant wave which inundates them simultaneously overwhelming 'all lives, all destinies'. The second passage has to do with definition, the speaker exploring the question at length when he observes that

> Being tall and shy, you can still stand up more clearly
> To the definition of what you are. You are not a sadist
> But must only trust in the dismantling of that definition
> Some day when names are being removed from things,
>   when all attributes
> Are sinking in the maelstrom of de-definition like spars.
> You must then come up with something to say,
> Anything as long as it's no more than five minutes long,
> And in the interval you shall have been washed. It's that easy.
> But meanwhile, I know, stone tenements are still hoarding
> The shadow that is mine; there is nothing to admit to,
> No one to confess to. This period goes on for quite a few years
> But as though along a low fence by a sidewalk. Then brandishes
> New definitions in its fists, but these are evidently false
> And get thrown out of court. Next you're on your own
> In an old film about two guys walking across the United States.
> The love that comes after will be richly satisfying,

> Like rain on the desert, calling unimaginable diplomacy into
>   being
> Until you thought you should get off here, maybe this stop
> Was yours.

(W, 84)

This is the history of a defining process, the speaker coming to terms with a definition of himself, dismantling it, abandoning himself to the 'maelstrom of de-definition', finding himself at the mercy of an aggressive re-definition, and finally, in a fond moment, seeming to imagine a scene 'two guys walking across the United States' in which definition was no longer an issue. This optimistic scene recalls the end of 'Palace Days', Ashbery, like White, offering an image of men comfortably identifying both with one another and also with 'we, yes, *we* Americans'.

Though it reaches for its setting into the past, the old movie suggesting, perhaps, a less troubled because more naive period, Ashbery's image looks forward to a period beyond definition made possible by an as yet 'unimaginable diplomacy'. The great achievement of 'A Wave' is in pointing us towards such a supple sensibility. It does so by developing two ideas from Auden: that 'suffering' takes place '[w]hile someone else is eating or opening a window or just walking dully along', and that 'We must love one another or die'. Ashbery builds the first idea into his the poem's shifting form. Line by line the poem resists definition because while it is sometimes concerned with an unnamed crisis, it is often taken up with eating, opening windows, or just walking dully along. The poem thus identifies a marginal community at risk, while always also being identifiable with the wider community of everyday life. Everyday life in Auden stands for indifference, whether as callousness as in 'Musée des Beaux Arts' or as universality as in 'September 1st 1939'. Ashbery's poem tends to move from the former meaning to the latter. Thus while, at the beginning of the poem, an image of suffering is offered only quickly to be disregarded in favour of more ordinary things and activities, the ending is an audible plea for human understanding:

> Please, it almost
> Seems to say, take me with you, I'm old enough. Exactly.
> And so each of us has to remain alone, conscious of each other
> Until the day when war absolves us of our differences. We'll
> Stay in touch. So they have it, all the time. But all was strange.
>
> (W, 89)

Crises such as wars absolve differences either because, in the face of the crisis, people mingle who would not ordinarily have contact with one another or because death is the great leveller. To avoid the cimmerian moment, this poem appears to argue, it is necessary to overcome the divisions which are a consequence of restrictive definitions. An unimaginable diplomacy is called into being.

NOTES

29. Shoptaw has an appendix charting the history of the poem's writing. The poem, which was begun in November 1982 and completed in 1983, went through six revisions, and in the process three titles: 'Landscape with Tobias and the Angel', 'Long Periods of Silence' and 'A Wave'. *On the Outside Looking Out*, pp. 343–351.

30. Shoptaw remarks that the 'ill-defined poem overwhelms its subjects'. *On the Outside Looking Out*, p. 277.

—David Herd, *John Ashbery and American Poetry* (New York: Palgrave, 2000): 202–205.

"At North Farm"

Although reticent to talk about his own work, Ashbery has written extensively about what he admires in his peers and forebears. Often, these pronouncements provide the clearest window into Ashbery's own poetics. *Other Traditions*, his six Norton lectures, is a perfect example. Another, especially as it relates to "At North Farm," is the following quote from a review of a Gertrude Stein volume that Ashbery wrote in 1957 for *Poetry* magazine:

> "*Stanzas in Meditation* gives one the feeling of time passing, of things happening, of a 'plot,' though it would be difficult to say precisely what is going on. Sometimes the story has the logic of a dream … while other times it becomes startlingly clear for a moment, as though a change in the wind had suddenly enabled us to hear a conversation that was taking place some distance away…. But it is usually not events which interest Miss Stein, rather it is their 'way of happening.'"

"At North Farm," the first poem in *A Wave* (1985), shares many of the same qualities that Ashbery praises in Stein, drawing on the allusive nature of familiar phrases, elliptical imagery, and dream logic to deconstruct and provoke the mind's fundamental need to arrange information into a narrative. As Paul Munn points out in one of the following critical extracts, the poem is a "vestigial sonnet" comprised of fourteen lines, which are broken into two verse paragraphs of six and eight lines, respectively, each with a different tone and emphasis. Gone, however, are the constraints of rhyme and meter. In their place, Ashbery employs refrain ("you" ending lines 4-6) and expressions so familiar they border on cliché. Yet couched in such an ambiguous context, common phrases such as "traveling furiously," "incredible speed," "day and night," "desert heat," "piled to the rafters," and "darken the sky" retain a paradoxical air of mystique, as if hiding something in plain view. Aiding this is Ashbery's trademark use of what he calls "the floating pronoun." Devoid of antecedents, "you," "we," and "him" are free to move about at will, assuming new identities with each reading, or else never taking shape at all, hovering on the margins of meaning like the liminal silhouettes of faces once familiar.

But not only the pronouns in "At North Farm" are floating. Many of the other words used are equally indefinite: somewhere, someone, where, thing, anything, here, sometimes, always, enough. There is something both familiar and unsettling about this colloquial lack of specificity, akin to blurry-edged dream settings and faceless personnel that we accept and interact with without needing to name. Though the title does refer to a specific mythical place from the Finnish folk epic, the *Kalevala*, a place near hell often described with the epithet "gloomy and prosperous," and though the poem's form is nominally a sonnet, these literary antecedents exist in the poem the same way as their missing grammatical equivalents—as ghostly echoes, undeniably present but resolutely equivocal. Detecting their traces can enrich a reader's appreciation for Ashbery's technique, but specific knowledge is in no way required to read and enjoy the poem and, in fact, an overemphasis on these sources would miss the point entirely. They are merely the couplings in the train of words and thoughts that emerges as an omen, an image, a feeling as readers runs it through the tunnel of their own associative filters. As such, it is enough to catch the drift of their presence, to create a mental picture of "North Farm" and to sort through the unsettling implications of a place where "hardly anything grows" and yet the "granaries are bursting with meal." Helen Vendler interprets this oxymoronic condition as a reference to the physical state of middle age, past one's prime and yet filled with a lifetime of memories and experience. It could just as easily refer to a poet full of ideas but unable to cull them into coherent expression, a love affair that has lost its spark, or any other situation in which a former bounty has gone mysteriously barren.

The structure of the poem mirrors this downshift. The first stanza is all momentum, the second all inertia. This contrast creates a compelling tension, an air of suspense that lingers, unresolved, long after the lines are read. Who is hunting us down, and why? What is the thing he has for us? For whom and what reason, exactly, are we leaving out a dish of milk? Is the gesture welcoming or apotropaic? Compelling questions, no doubt, but, like Stein's *Stanzas in Meditation*, the poem is less interested in providing answers—a specific plot or subject matter—than it is in exploring the "mixed feelings" that arise between text and meaning, familiar and other. Ultimately, it is up to the reader to determine whether this is "enough."

CRITICAL VIEWS ON
"At North Farm"

Helen Vendler on Death and American Diction

[Helen Vendler is an eminent critic and Professor of English at Harvard University. Her many publications include the National Book Critics Circle Award-winning *Part of Nature, Part of Us: Modern American Poetry*, as well as *Soul Says: On Recent Poetry* and *The Given and The Made: Strategies of Poetic Redefinition*. In the following excerpt from another collection of essays on modern poetics, Vendler identifies Death as the unnamed pursuer in the poem and praises Ashbery's effective use of the vernacular.]

The figures traced in John Ashbery's rich book *A Wave* (1984) have to do with death: in fact, *A Wave* has qualities of a last testament. As I first read the opening poem, "At North Farm" (the Farm is from the *Kalevala*), it seemed to me a poem about the Angel of Death:

> Somewhere someone is traveling furiously toward you,
> At incredible speed, traveling day and night,
> Through blizzards and desert heat, across torrents, through
>   narrow passes.
> But will he know where to find you,
> Recognize you when he sees you,
> Give you the thing he has for you?
>
> Hardly anything grows here,
> Yet the granaries are bursting with meal,
> The sacks of meal piled to the rafters.
> The streams run with sweetness, fattening fish;
> Birds darken the sky. Is it enough
> That the dish of milk is set out at night,
> That we think of him sometimes,
> Sometimes and always, with mixed feelings?

We register at first the clichés, as we read "incredible speed," "desert heat," "narrow passes," "granaries ... bursting," and "mixed feelings." These trip so easily on the tongue that we understand this drama to be something "everyone knows": and yet at the same time the paradoxes of drought and abundance, sweetness and menace, dread and longing, warn us that this is an almost unimaginable state of affairs. Someone travels furiously toward you (with all the determination of the Post Office)—but will he—and here the poem takes its cue from the catchiness of popular lyric, "know where to find you ... when he sees you ... give you the thing he has for you?" Ashbery has said that this is the messenger of love, not death, but perhaps one can call him Fate, of whom we always think with mixed feelings.

No pleasure is sweeter in the ear than something new done to the old. Ashbery's deep literary dependencies escape cliche by the pure Americanness of his diction. A middle-aged American reads "Hardly anything grows here" with immediate recognition, a shock not possible any longer from the mention in a contemporary poem of "stubble plains" or "the barrenness / Of the fertile thing that can attain no more"—words used so memorably that they cannot be reused. Ashbery's gift for American plainness is his strongest weapon: "Hardly anything grows here" disarms us in its naked truth.

At the same time, in barren middle age one has seen too much; there is more experience than one can ever consume in recollection or perpetuate in art—the granaries are bursting with meal. That too, while Keatsian, is American in its "bursting with meal" (in Keats, what burst are clouds, in tears). Ashbery's propitiatory dish of milk for the goblin (to keep him outside the house) is just unexpected enough, as folk naiveté, to throw us off balance (in this Keatsian, Stevensian context); it gives us Fate through the lens of the literary grotesque instead of through the lens of tragicomic destiny (traveling furiously) or the lens of seasonal turn (vegetative barrenness, harvest plenty). Will it keep Fate out of the house if we set milk out for him? (Milton: "The drudging Goblin sweat, / To earn his cream-bowl duly set.") Will it mollify the Goblin if we don't think badly of him? And yet, isn't there as well a hope that he will come and stop for us and give us what he has for us—the horoscope in his hand? Emily Dickinson,

whose air of macabre comedy often resembles Ashbery's, would
have read this poem with perfect comprehension.

—Helen Vendler, *The Music of What Happens: Poems, Poets, Critics*
(Cambridge: Harvard University Press, 1988): 252–254.

PAUL MUNN ON VESTIGIAL FORM

[Paul Munn is a Professor of English at Saginaw Valley
State University and the author of numerous articles on
Ashbery and other modern poets. This extract presents
Munn's own interpretation of the poem as a "vestigial
sonnet."]

The poetry of John Ashbery has become a lightning rod for
major critics of contemporary poetry. Harold Bloom, Marjorie
Perloff, and Charles Altieri, for example, have variously
emphasized Ashbery's anxious responses to poetic, especially
Romantic, precursors; his indeterminacy in "the other tradition"
of the French Symbolists; or his complex postmodernism in
contrast to a simpler scenic mode.[1] Not wrangling directly with
any of these views, I wish to defend a modest claim about three
poems in his 1984 volume, *A Wave*: Ashbery's vestigial forms
suggest a poet who, however anxious and indeterminate in many
poems, is capable in some poems of a rhetorically
comprehensible use of poetic form, however complex and
ingenious.[2] In three poems, Ashbery's vestigial forms suggest
three related poets: an almost comfortably conventional
sonneteer, an ironic usurper of the English hymn, and a witty
remaker of the Japanese haibun.[3]

A Wave is composed of forty-four poems, counting his "37
Haiku" as one. Twenty-seven of these are what most would call
"free verse," what Lewis Turco, I believe, would call poetry in the
mode of lineated prose. Three are prose poems, unlineated
poetry. The remaining fourteen are poems written in what I have
chosen to call vestigial form, poems that recall to some
significant degree visual and other devices of poetic artifice with
substantial conventional precedent, such as rhymed couplets,
sonnets, quatrains, haiku, and haibun. I might have called the

perceived form in these fourteen poems echoic form, tendentious form, threshold form, gestural form, subdued form, marginal form, or fossilized form—all these rubrics are near synonyms for vestigial form, each placing a different emphasis on how form appears to us.

The label "vestigial form," though it has perhaps the disadvantage of suggesting too strongly the organic and the nonfunctional, has the virtue of evoking connotations of genetic links with the past, a visible and rudimentary trace of a more vigorous preceding generation. Like little toes on the human foot, once very useful to our barefoot ancestors, vestigial poetic forms serve to remind us of previous purposes. But little toes are still somewhat useful: they do provide some balance, and on the beach or in the bed, they may function or entertain. Similarly, vestigial forms contribute subtly to poetic meaning. Primarily, they invite us to apply the conventions of lyric poetry in general. But they may also invite us to make meaning by considering the conventions of a particular antecedent form. This is the case in three Ashbery poems in which vestiges of the sonnet, the quatrain, and the Japanese haibun appear.

"At North Farm," the first poem in *A Wave*, directly preceding another poem of fourteen lines, is a vestigial sonnet:

> Somewhere someone is traveling furiously toward you,
> At incredible speed, traveling day and night,
> Through blizzards and desert heat, across torrents, through
> narrow passes.
> But will he know where to find you,
> Recognize you when he sees you,
> Give you the thing he has for you?
>
> Hardly anything grows here,
> Yet the granaries are bursting with meal,
> The sacks of meal piled to the rafters.
> The streams run with sweetness, fattening fish;
> Birds darken the sky. Is it enough
> That the dish of milk is set out at night,
> That we think of him sometimes,
> Sometimes and always, with mixed feelings?

The first verse paragraph is six lines; the second is eight lines, suggesting an inverted Italian sonnet, its slightly uneven bipartite form quite conventionally suggesting "build-up" in the first part and "release" of "pressure" in the second part.[4] More resistant than traditional sonnets to translation into prose paraphrase, the poem nevertheless—like fine examples of the Italian sonnet in Milton, Wordsworth, Keats, and Auden—uses the two-part formal asymmetry to reinforce a significant shift in scene, idea, or mood. The first part creates a feeling of mysterious activity. We wonder at the nature of the errand of the unknown furious traveler. The second part creates a contrasting feeling of stasis and inexplicable fruition. From a hazardous landscape we shift to "here" (l. 7), "At North Farm," we suspect, where the landscape has been domesticated for cultivation, where the activities are habitual, not hazardous, where farmers harvest, and, customarily and superstitiously, "the dish of milk is set out at night."

In spite of the inversion of the length of the two parts and lack of rhyme, this poem is, in its intervolvement of form and theme, almost comfortably conventional. Five-stress or decasyllabic lines occur (2, 8, 10, 12), vestiges of the pentameter line of the sonnet in English.[5] Although the poem lacks end rhyme, it abounds in traditional devices of lyric poetry, contributing to the urgency of tone in the first part and the atmosphere of stasis in the second: repeated words, internal rhyme, alliteration, assonance, and consonance. It is a poem about a relationship between one person and another person or persons who perceive him as at once menacing and alluring, and its subject and tone emerge as part of the artifice of the vestigial sonnet. I say "almost" because Ashbery's pronouns create a strangely dislocated fictional utterance as we attempt to make meaning and connect the two parts of the poem. And the poem as introduction to a book of poems suggests perhaps a menacing and alluring poet who through his words travels furiously toward his readers and leaves us indeed with "mixed feelings."

The title of a later poem in *A Wave* asks a question that applies to Ashbery's work generally and to the role of form in his work: "But What Is the Reader to Make of This?" The answer to the question of the role of vestigial form in "At North Farm," I believe, emerges when one sees the similarity between the achievement of the Renaissance lyric, including the sonnet, and what Ashbery states as the goal of his poetic art. David Kalstone, writing on Sir Philip Sidney's *Astrophel and Stella*, tells us, "The movement of mind, so often praised in Donne, is already present in many of the sonnets of Sidney's sequence."[6] Ashbery, commenting on his use of what he calls "the floating pronoun," tells us, "I'm interested in the movement of the mind, how it goes from one place to the other and the places themselves don't matter that much. It's the movement that does" (Munn, "Interview" 62). However "indeterminate" Ashbery often appears, his words here suggest that he attempts to do what the greatest Renaissance lyricists attempted to do, to imitate human consciousness more realistically through poetic artifice, not to describe or transcribe but to render experience in language. "At North Farm" is a participant, however belated and estranged, in a formal tradition that has, since its introduction into English in the Renaissance, imitated mental movement.

NOTES

1. Altieri has also identified in Ashbery and other poets what he calls "rhetoricity ... the complex states of mind that go into self-conscious manipulation of language" (*Self and Sensibility in Contemporary American Poetry* [Cambridge: Cambridge Univ. Press, 1984] 146). Recently, James McCorkle has explored in Ashbery and others poetic "interconnection [which] is the means of engaging the phenomenal world and implies a reinvention of the self that can engage a variety of voices, fragments, and inadvertent glimpses" (*The Still Performance: Writing, Self, and Interconnection in Five Postmodern American Poets* [Charlottesville: Univ. Press of Virginia, 1989] 4).

2. *A Wave: Poems by John Ashbery* (New York: Penguin, 1984).

3. Richard Howard observes Ashbery's career moving from conventional forms (his virtual first volume, *Some Trees*, 1956, included poems titled "Eclogue," "Canzone," "Sonnet," and "Pantoum," as well as three sestinas) through the prose poems of *Three Poems*, 1972. *Self-Portrait in a Convex Mirror*, 1975, is representative of what Howard calls "a prosody ... of intermittence and collage; no such conventional markings as rhyme or repetition—rather, *seamless verse*, jammed rather than enjambed, extended rather than intense; it must go on and on to keep the whole contraption from coming round again, to work upon us its deepest effect, which is a kind of snake-charming" ("John Ashbery," in *John Ashbery: Modern Critical Views*, ed. Harold Bloom [New York: Chelsea, 1985] 45). But *Houseboat Days*, 1981, is a fifty-poem sequence, each poem four unrhymed quatrains. Ashbery's flamboyant experimentalism throughout his

career often invoked conventional forms, and the concept of vestigial form often usefully applies to Ashbery's earlier work and to his *April Galleons*, 1987, which includes poems in paired lines, four-line stanzas, and five-line stanzas.

4. Paul Fussell, *Poetic Meter and Poetic Form*, rev. ed. (New York: Random House, 1979) 116.

5. Ashbery has said, "I don't much like sonnets" ("An Interview with John Ashbery," with John Koethe, *SubStance* 37/38 [1983]: 178–86, 183). In his interview with me, he observed that sonnets and certain other "forms ... are really too loose to have this liberating effect that I'm looking for, especially in teaching" ("An Interview with John Ashbery," *New Orleans Review* 17.2 [Summer 1990]: 59–63, 62). But these statements do not at all preclude his writing a vestigial sonnet, a transformation of the form suited to particular ends similar to the ends of its antecedents.

6. "Sir Philip Sidney," *English Poetry and Prose, 1540–1674*, ed. Christopher Ricks (London: Barrie & Jenkins, 1970), 41–59, 56. Kalstone also contributes to criticism of Ashbery: "*Self-Portrait in A Convex Mirror*," in *John Ashbery: Modern Critical Views*, ed. Harold Bloom (New York: Chelsea, 1985) 91–114.

—Paul Munn. "Vestigial Form in John Ashbery's A Wave," *New Orleans Review* 19:1 (Spring 1992): 19–21

John Shoptaw on Ashbery's Mode of Production

[In another extract from his book on Ashbery, Shoptaw investigates an early draft of the poem as a means of unearthing its elliptical framework.]

This lucid but indeterminate poem exemplifies what Marjorie Perloff has termed the "poetics of indeterminacy." The poem raises a host of questions: Who is traveling toward "you"? Does "you" mean "we" or Ashbery or someone else? Is it singular or plural, specific or general? Where is "Somewhere" and "here"? Is there an allegorical significance to the pastoral details? The poem doesn't provide us with enough consistent information to answer such basic reading questions. As Perloff says of "Rivers and Mountains," "The reader can invent any number of plots and locations that fit this 'all-purpose model.'"[29]

But although we cannot determine any single plot or subject for the poem, we can identify the representational, relational system which produced it, and through which its particulars circulate. This does not mean, however, that Ashbery is a systematic poet. In a 1977 interview Ashbery took pains to argue that there "is no systematic rationale or systematic anything in my poetry. If it is systematic, it's only in its total avoidance of any kind of system or program."[30] His Vietnam-era prose poem "The System" associates his anti-systematic method with the demise of the Establishment: "The system was breaking down" (TP 53). Yet for all Ashbery's resistance to self-conscious, systematic poetic production, it becomes increasingly apparent that his poems are kept afloat by the systems into which their sender unknowingly enters. He puts it paradoxically in his long poem "A Wave": "By so many systems / As we are involved in, by just so many / Are we set free on an ocean of language that comes to be / Part of us, as though we would ever get away" (W 71). In my discussions of Ashbery's poems, I locate their meaning in their mode of production. My readings are thus not "close" but textually specific. Rather than considering poems "as such," I examine how they misrepresent and reformulate the various systems of discourses, texts, and practices within which they are produced.

Ashbery's gradual realization of "At North Farm" is revealed in the typescript. Though the poem ends up as an unrhymed inverted sonnet, its twelve typewritten lines show that Ashbery didn't begin with this idea in mind (and may not have noticed it at all). Only after drafting the poem on the typewriter did he write in the title (while Ashbery often begins with a title, sometimes recycled from the titles of unpublished poems, he just as often ends with it, as though he discovered the subject of his poem by writing it). He also specified his core narrative of travel and delivery with a handwritten allusion in what is now the poem's third, long-distance line, which misrepresents the postman's motto, translated from Herodotus (*Histories*, VIII, 98), and inscribed on the New York City Post Office: "Neither snow, nor rain, nor heat, nor gloom of night stays these couriers from the swift completion of their appointed rounds." The allusion differs significantly from those we might find in *The Waste Land* or *The Cantos*. It is typically Ashberian in that it refers us to our common knowledge and language: to understand the postman's motto, we need not know its origin in Herodotus, only its popularly recycled version, once on the lips of every American schoolchild. When his allusions are obscure, they tend to misrepresent familiar sources; our understanding of the title "On First Listening to Schreker's *Der Schatzgräber*" (ATS 58), for instance, depends not on our knowing this piece of music but on our hearing the distorted echo of Keats's "On First Looking into Chapman's Homer." The narrative system of "At North Farm," which I will call the postal or communications system, is common in Ashbery poems, especially those featuring the pronoun "you," the destination of four of the poem's first six lines. This relational network requires a messenger (who may also be the sender), a message, and a receiver.[31] The first stanza of "At North Farm" locates itself in the "Somewhere" of the approaching messenger, the second in the "here" of the waiting receiver. We can generate different readings of "At North Farm" depending on what details we select. Taking "you" as Ashbery's readers, and "we" as the autumnal, expectant poet waiting along with us, we may read the poem self-reflexively as the advent of a new poem or of *A Wave* itself. Or we may take "someone ... traveling" at the speed of light to be God's "incredible" messenger, Christ (or Santa; the poem was written between Christmas and New Year's eve) with his gifts. Or "we may think of him" with "mixed feelings" as Death, whom we perhaps put off with an apotropaic "dish of milk." Or "he" may be a new or returning lover, drawn by the milk like a stray tomcat. Any of these readings is possible, yet none of them accounts for all the particulars in the poem. But if the details change at "incredible speed," the postal system keeps them in circulation.

Ashbery drew both the characteristic syntax and the title of "At North Farm" from *The Kalevala*, a collection of Finnish oral epic poems. Its varied repetitions—"But will he know where to find you, / Recognize you when he sees you," "Yet the granaries are bursting with meal, / The sacks of meal piled to the rafters"— are patterned on the paraphrastic parallelisms characteristic of the Finnish epic.[32] North Farm, as Ashbery has explained, is "a place referred to frequently in that poem, with the epithet 'gloomy and prosperous north farm.' ... It's situated somewhere near hell."[33] The mainstay of the North Farm economy is a truly indispensable appliance known as the Sampo: "it ground a binful in the dawn, one binful of things to eat; / it ground a second of things to sell, a third of household supplies" (p. 60). Ashbery remarked that "the plenty alluded to" in his own poem "has an unnatural origin, some magical reason for being there, since it didn't grow there."[34] "At North Farm" is itself a Sampo, mashing the slack paraphrases of the oral epic and the courtly concision of the sonnet into a typically misrepresentative mixture of poetic kinds.

The mixture is homotextual. In *The Kalevala*, North Farm is the region where heroes travel in search of wives. Ashbery has described his messenger as "a lover, perhaps of a somewhat ominous kind that would remind one of mortality,"[35] thus locating himself, along with us, "here" at North Farm in the wife's receiving position. In this regard "At North Farm" recalls Auden's famous rendition of the Anglo-Saxon lyric "The Wanderer": "But ever that man goes / Through place-keepers, through forest trees, / A stranger to strangers over undried sea, / Houses for fishes, suffocating water" (EA 55). The similarities between the two poems are manifold (both employ the syntax of variant repetition, both adopt an Anglo-Saxon alliterative stress meter, both are well stocked with fish and restless birds), but "The Wanderer" resembles "At North Farm" most crucially in its homotextual displacements. Auden's poem plumbs the unfathomable destiny of sexual orientation, a "Doom ... dark and deeper than any sea-dingle." In Auden's version, the wanderer, exiled from his wife, dreams of her "Waving from window, spread of welcome," and wakes among sea-birds and "new men making another love" (EA 55). But in the Old English poem, the wanderer's "wife" (never specified by Auden as "she") is his liege-lord, who inexplicably banished him to the wrenching frustration of his dream: "Often, when grief and sleep combined together enchain the wretched solitary man, it seems to him in his imagination that he is embracing and kissing his lord and laying hands and head on his knee.... Then the friendless man awakes again and sees before him tawny waves, sea-birds bathing, spreading their wings, rime falling and snow, mingled with hail."[36] As the paranoid exile of Ashbery's "Worsening Situation" confides: "My wife / Thinks I'm in Oslo—Oslo, France, that is" (SP 4). Like "Oslo" and "France," "I" and "my wife" intersect only in the poem. In an unpublished, untitled fragment beginning "Dame Shadows brought me a present," Ashbery considers his homotextual use of his second person: "Difficult to write this: you, of course, is not my wife—I have no wife: / It is a man, presently asleep, whom I have known for some time but not too well." Such moments of determinate attribution are rare in Ashbery's poetry, published or not; his second-person pronouns function most commonly as homotextual variables within his all-purpose systems.

NOTES

29. Marjorie Perloff, *The Poetics of Indeterminacy: Rimbaud to Cage* (1981; Chicago: Northwestern UP, 1983) 254.

30. David Lehman, "A Conversation with John Ashbery" unpublished interview, 17 October 1977: 6.

31. This system resembles the actantial model of narrative developed by Algirdas Greimas, with its sender, helper, subject, object, opponent, and receiver, and Roman Jakobson's model of literary reception, with its addresser, context, message, contact, code, and addressee. See Algirdas Julien Greimas, *Structural Semantics: An Attempt at a Method*, trans. Daniele McDowell, Ronald Schleifer, and Alan Velie (Lincoln: Nebraska UP, 1983); Roman Jakobson, "Linguistics and Poetics," *Language in Literature* (Cambridge: Harvard UP, 1987) 62–94.

32. *The Kalevala: or Poems of the Kaleva District*, trans. Francis Peabody Magoun, Jr. (Cambridge: Harvard UP, 1963). Ashbery read this edition.

33. Quoted in David Lehman, "John Ashbery: The Pleasures of Poetry," *The New York Times Magazine* 16 Dec. 1984: 84.

34. Lehman 84.

35. Lehman 84. See Helen Vendler, *The Music of What Happens: Poems, Poets, Critics* (Cambridge: Harvard UP, 1988) 252–54: "Ashbery has said that this is the messenger of love, not death, but perhaps one can call him Fate, of whom we always think with mixed feelings" (253).

36. "The Wanderer," *Anglo-Saxon Poetry*, trans. and ed. S. A. J. Bradley (London: Dent, 1982) 323.

—John Shoptaw, *On the Outside Looking Out* (Cambridge: Harvard Univ. Press, 1994): 10–13

WORKS BY

John Ashbery

Turandot and Other Poems, 1953.

Some Trees, 1956.

The Poems, 1960.

The Tennis Court Oath, 1962.

Rivers and Mountains, 1966.

Sunrise in Suburbia, 1968.

The American Literary Anthology, ed., 1968.

Three Madrigals, 1968.

Fragment, 1969.

A Nest of Ninnies, 1969 (with James Schuyler).

The Double Dream of Spring, 1970.

The New Spirit, 1970.

Three Poems, 1972.

Penguin Modern Poets 24, ed., 1974.

The Vermont Notebook, 1975 (with Joe Brainard).

Self-Portrait in a Convex Mirror, 1975.

Houseboat Days, 1977.

Three Plays, 1978.

As We Know, 1979.

Kitaj, 1981 (with R.B. Kitaj).

Shadow Train, 1981.

Fairfield Porter, 1982 (with others).

A Wave, 1985.

Selected Poems, 1985.

April Galleons, 1987.

The Ice Storm, 1987.

Selected Poems, 1987.

Reported Sightings: Art Chronicles 1957–1987, 1989 (ed. by
D. Bergman).

Flow Chart, 1991.

Selected Poems: Pierre Reverdy, 1991 (with M.A. Caws, P. Terry).

Hotel Lautréamont, 1992.

Three Books, 1993.

And The Stars Were Shining, 1994.

Can You Hear Birds, 1995.

The Mooring of Starting Out, 1997.

Girls on the Run, 1999.

Other Traditions, 2000.

Your Name Here: Poems, 2000.

As Umbrellas Follow Rain, 2001.

Chinese Whispers, 2002.

WORKS ABOUT

John Ashbery

Altieri, Charles. "John Ashbery in Britain: A Supplement." *PN Review* 21:1 (Sept–Oct 1994): 32–81.

———. "Motives in Metaphor: John Ashbery and the Modernist Long Poem." *Genre* 11 (Winter 1978): 653–687.

———. *Self and Sensibility in Contemporary American Poetry.* Cambridge: Cambridge University Press, 1984.

———. "John Ashbery and the Challenge of Postmodernism in the Visual Arts." *Critical Inquiry* 14:4 (Summer 1988): 805–30.

———. "Ashbery as Love Poet." *Verse* 8:1 (Spring 1991): 8–15.

Applewhite, James. "Painting, Poetry, Abstraction, and Ashbery." *The Southern Review* 24:2 (Spring 1988): 272–290.

Blasing, Mutlu Konuk. *American Poetry: The Rhetoric of Its Forms.* New Haven: Yale University Press, 1987

———. *Politics and Form in Postmodern Poetry: O'Hara, Bishop, Ashbery, and Merrill.* Cambridge: Cambridge University Press, 1995.

Bloom, Harold. *Figures of Capable Imagination.* New York: The Seabury Press, 1976.

———. *Agon: Towards a Theory of Revisionism.* New York: Oxford University Press, 1982.

———, ed. *Deconstruction and Criticism.* New York: Continuum, 1979.

———, ed. *Modern Critical Views: John Ashbery.* New York: Chelsea House Publishers, 1985.

Bromwich, David. "John Ashbery: The Self Against Its Images." *Raritan* 5:4 (Spring 1986): 36–58.

Costello, Bonnie. "John Ashbery and the Idea of the Reader." *Contemporary Literature* 23 (Fall 1982): 493–514.

Clark, Kevin. "'A Wave': Privileging the Symbol." *Papers on Language & Literature* 26:2 (Spring 1990): 271–279.

Dayan, Joan. "Finding What Will Suffice: John Ashbery's *A Wave*." *Modern Language Notes* 100:5 (December 1985): 1045–1079.

Di Piero, W.S. "John Ashbery: The Romantic as Problem Solver." *American Poetry Review* (July/August 1973): 39–42.

Edelman, Lee. "The Pose of Imposture: Ashbery's 'Self-Portrait in a Convex Mirror'." *Twentieth Century Literature* 32:1 (Spring 1986): 95–114.

Erwin, John W. "The Reader is the Medium: Ashbery and Ammons Ensphered." *Contemporary Literature* 21:4 (1980): 588–610.

Fink, Thomas. "'Here and There' The Locus of Language in John Ashbery's 'Self-Portrait in a Convex Mirror'." *Contemporary Poetry* 4:3 (1982): 47–64.

———."The Comic Thrust of Ashbery's Poetry." *Twentieth Century Literature* 30 (1984): 1–14.

Fite, David. "John Ashbery: The Effort to Make Sense." *Mississippi Review* 2:2 (Spring 1979): 123–30.

———. "On the Virtues of Modesty: John Ashbery's Tactics against Transcendence." *Modern Language Quarterly* 42 (1981): 78–79.

Gardner, Thomas. "'You Can't Live There': Ashbery's 'Self-Portrait in a Convex Mirror,'" *Poesis* 7:2 (1986): 57–77.

———. *Discovering Ourselves in Whitman: The Contemporary American Long Poem*. Urbana: University of Illinois Press, 1989.

———. *Regions of Unlikeness: Explaining Contemporary Poetry*. Lincoln: University of Nebraska Press, 1999.

Heffernan, James A. W. *Museum of Words: The Poetics of Ekphrasis from Homer to Ashbery*. Chicago: University of Chicago Press, 1993.

Herd, David. "'When Time Shall Force a Gift on Each': Ashbery, Pasternak and Avant-Garde Expression." *Critical Quarterly* 40:4 (1998): 47–64.

———. *John Ashbery and American Poetry*. New York: Palgrave, 2000.

Hoeppner, Edward Haworth. *Echoes and Moving Fields: Structure and Subjectivity in the Poetry of W. S. Merwin and John Ashbery.* Lewisburg: Bucknell University Press, 1994.

Jackson, Richard. "Writing as Transgression: Ashbery's Archeology of the Moment," *Southern Humanities Review* 12:3 (Summer 1978): 279–283.

Kalstone, David. *Five Temperaments.* Oxford: Oxford University Press, 1977.

Kelly, Lionel, ed. *Poetry and the Sense of Panic: Critical Essays on Elizabeth Bishop and John Ashbery.* Amsterdam: Editions Rodopi B.V., 2000.

Kerman, David. *John Ashbery: A Comprehensive Bibliography (Including His Art Criticism, and with Selected Notes from Unpublished Materials).* New York: Garland Publishing, 1976.

Kinzie, Mary. "The Poetic Diction of John Ashbery." *Modern Philology* 82 (1981): 267–82; 382–400.

Leckie, Ross. "Art, Mimesis, and John Ashbery's 'Self-Portrait in a Convex Mirror'." *Essays in Literature* 19:1 (Sprint 1992): 114–131.

Lehman, David, ed. *Beyond Amazement: New Essays on John Ashbery.* Ithaca: Cornell University Press, 1980.

———. *The Last Avant-Garde: The Making of the New York School of Poets.* New York: Doubleday, 1998

Lieberman, Laurence. *Unassigned Frequencies: American Poetry in Review, 1964–77.* Urbana: University of Illinois Press, 1964: pp. 3–61.

Malinowska, Barbara. *Dynamics of Being, Space, and Time in the Poetry of Czesław Miłosz and John Ashbery.* New York: Peter Lang, 2000.

McClatchy, J. D. *White Paper on Contemporary American Poetry.* New York: Columbia University Press, 1989.

McCorkle, James. *The Still Performance: Writing, Self and Interconnection.* Charlottesville: University of Virginia Press, 1989.

Meyer, Steven. "Ashbery: Poet for All Seasons." *Raritan* 15:2 (Fall 1995): 144–161.

Miklitsch, Robert. "John Ashbery." *Contemporary Literature* 21:1 (Winter 1980): 118–135.

Miller, S.H. "Psychic Geometry: John Ashbery's Prose Poems." *American Poetry* 3:1 (Fall 1985): 24–42.

Mills-Courts, Karen. *Poetry as Epitaph: Representation and Poetic Language*. Baton Rouge: Lousiana State University Press, 1990.

Moramarco, Fred. "John Ashbery and Frank O'Hara: The Painterly Poets." *Journal of Modern Literature* 5 (September 1976): 436–62.

Mueller, Robert. "John Ashbery and the Poetry of Consciousness: 'Self-Portrait in a Convex Mirror'." *The Centennial Review* 40:3 (Fall 1996): 561–572.

Munn, Paul. "An Interview with John Ashbery." *New Orleans Review* 17:2 (Summer 1990): 59–93.

———. "Vestigial Form in John Ashbery's *A Wave*," *New Orleans Review* 19:1 (Spring 1992): 19–21

Myers, John Bernard, ed. *The Poets of the New York School*. Philadelphia: University of Pennsylvania Press, 1969.

Norton, Jody. "'Whispers Out of Time': The Syntax of Being in the Poetry of John Ashbery." *Twentieth Century Literature* 41:3 (Fall 1995): 281–305.

———. *Narcisuss* Sous Rature: *Male Subjectivity in Contemporary American Poetry*, 2000.

Perloff, Marjorie. "'Transparent Selves': The Poetry of John Ashbery and Frank O'Hara." *The Yearbook of English Studies* 8 (1978): 171–196.

———. *The Poetics of Indeterminacy: Rimbaud to Cage*. Princeton: Princeton University Press, 1981.

———. *Poetic License: Essays on Modernist and Postmodernist Lyric*. Evanston: Northwestern University Press, 1990.

———. *Radical Artifice: Writing in the Age of Media*. Chicago: University of Chicago Press, 1991.

Schultz, Susan, ed. *The Tribe of John: Ashbery and Contemporary Poetry*. Tuscaloosa: The University of Alabama Press, 1995.

Shapiro, David. *John Ashbery: An Introduction to the Poetry*. New York: Columbia University Press, 1979.

Shoptaw, John. *On the Outside Looking Out: John Ashbery's Poetry*. Cambridge: Harvard University Press, 1994.

Spurr, David. "John Ashbery's Poetry of Language." *Centennial Review* 25:2 (1981): pp 156–161.

Stamelman, Richard. "Critical Reflections: Poetry and Art Criticism in Ashbery's 'Self-Portrait in a Convex Mirror'." *New Literary History* 15:3 (Spring 1984): 607–630.

Stitt, Peter. *Uncertainty & Plenitude: Five Contemporary Poets*. Iowa City: University of Iows Press, 1997.

Vendler, Helen. "Understanding Ashbery." *New Yorker* (March 16, 1981): 119–135.

———. "Making it New." *New York Review of Books* 31:10 (June 14, 1984): 32–34.

———. *The Music of What Happens: Poems, Poets, Critics*. Cambridge: Harvard University Press, 1988.

———. *The Given and the Made: Recent American Poets*. London: Faber and Faber, 1995.

Ward, Geoff. *Statutes of Liberty: The New York School of Poets*. New York: Palgrave, 1993.

Wilson, Rob. "John Ashbery's Post-Industrial Sublime." *Verse* 8:1 (Spring 1991): 48–52.

Zinnes, Harriet. "John Ashbery: The Way Time Feels as it Passes." *Hollins Critic* 29:3 (June 1992): 1–13.

ACKNOWLEDGMENTS

"Vision in the Form of a Task: 'The Double Dream of Spring'" by Charles Berger. From *Beyond Amazement: New Essays on John Ashbery*, edited by David Lehman. Copyright © 1980 by Cornell University. Used by permission of the publisher, Cornell University Press.

"Soonest Mended" by John Hollander. From *The Work of Poetry* by John Hollander. © 1997 by Columbia Uiversity Press. Reprinted by permission.

"The Charity of the Hard Moments" by Harold Bloom. From *Figures of Capable Imagination*. Copyright © 1976 by Harold Bloom. Reprinted by permission of the author.

"John Ashbery's Difficulty" by Vernon Shetley. From *After the Death of Poetry*. © 1993 by Duke University Press. Pp. 110–116. All rights reserved. Used by permission of the publisher.

"Forms of action: experiment and declaration in *Rivers and Mountains and The Double Dream of Spring*" by David Herd. From *John Ashbery and American Poetry*. Pp. 119–121; 202–205. © David Herd 2000. Reprinted by permission.

"Self-Portrait in a Convex Mirror" by David Kalstone. From *Five Temperaments*. © 1977 by David Kalstone and Oxford University Press. Reprinted by permission.

"Critical Reflections" by Richard Stamelman. From *New Literary History* vol. xv, no. 3 (Spring 1984): pp. 613–616. © 1984 by Johns Hopkins University Press. Reprinted by permission.

"A Comission That Never Materialized": Narcissism and Lucidity in Ashbery's 'Self Portrait in a Convex Mirror'" by Anita Sokolsky. © 1985 by Anita Sokolsky. From *Modern Critical Views: John Ashbury*, edited by Harold Bloom. Reprinted by permission of the author.

"The Pose of Imposture: Ashbury's 'Self-Portrait in a Convex Mirror'" by Lee Edelman. From *Twentieth Century Literature* 32: 1 (Spring 1986): pp. 95–99. © 1986 by Hofstra University Press. Reprinted by permission.

A Metaphor Made to Include Us: John Ashbery's "self Portrait in a Convex Mirror'" by Thomas Gardner. From *Discovering Ourselves in Whitman*. Pp. 148–152. © 1989 by Thomas Gardner. Reprinted by permission.

"Measuring the Canon: 'Wet Casements' and 'Tapestry'" by Harold Bloom. From *Agon*. © 1982 by Oxford University Press. Reprinted by permission.

"John Ashbery" by David Bromwich. From *Raritan* 5:4 (Spring 1986): pp. 36–41; 54–57. © 1986 by Rutgers University Press. Reprinted by permission from Raritan: A Quarterly Review, Vol. V, No. 4 (Spring 1986).

"The Thing for Which There is No Name" by Karen Mills-Courts. From *Poetry as Epitaph*. Pp. 279–284. © 1990 by Lousiana State University Press. Reprinted by permission.

"Houseboat Days" by John Shoptaw. From *On the Outside Looking Out*. Pp. 199–201. © 1994 by the president and fellows of Harvard College. Reprinted by permission.

"Ashbery and Influence" by Geoff Ward. From *Statutes of Liberty: The New York School of Poets*. Pp. 130–134.© 1993, 2001 by Geoff Ward. Reprinted by permission.

"Writing As Transgression: Ashbery's Ercheology of the Moment—A Review" by Richard Jackson. From *Southern Humanities Review* 13:3 (Summer 1978):pp. 279–284. © 1978 by Richard Jackson. Reprinted by permission.

"Syringa" by Lawrence Kramer. From *Beyond Amazement: New Essays on John Ashbery*. Pp. 256–259. © 1980 by Cornell University Press. Used by permission of the publisher, Cornell University Press.

"Houseboat Days" by John Shoptaw. From On the Outside Looking Out. Pp. 10–13; 209–212. © 1994 by the president and fellows of Harvard College. Reprinted by permission.

"Finding What Will Suffice: John Ashbery's A Wave" by Joan Dayan. From *Modern Language Notes: Comparative Literature* 100:5 (December 1985): pp. 1045–1046; 1064–1067. © 1985

INDEX OF
Themes and Ideas